Ski Trails of Southwest Montana

30 of the Best Cross Country and Snowshoe Trails around Big Sky, Bozeman & Paradise Valley

Melynda Harrison

with Trail Maps by

Mariann Van Den Elzen

Greater Yellowstone Ski Trails

Volume 1

PRESS

First Ascent Press

Livingston, MT

Disclaimer

There are no warranties, whether expressed or implied, that this guidebook is accurate or that the information contained in it is reliable. Your use of this book indicates your assumption of the risk that it may contain errors and is an acknowledgment of your sole responsibility for your skiing and winter safety.

First Ascent Press, LLC
PO Box 2338
Livingston, MT 59047

PRESS   www.firstascentpress.com

Ski Trails of Southwest Montana
by Melynda Harrison
with Trail Maps by Mariann Van Den Elzen

Greater Yellowstone Ski Trails
Volume 1

Library of Congress Control Number: 2007936270
ISBN 13: 978-1-933009-148
ISBN 10: 1-933009-144

11   10   09   08   07   2   3   4   5   6   7   8   9   10

Front Cover Photo: Ski touring near Big Sky, Montana. Photo © Bob Allen Photography.
Back Cover Photo: Snowshoeing in the Bridger Range. Photo © Bob Allen Photography.

The Author and Publisher would like to acknowledge and thank Bob and Estela Allen Photography, Tristin Dunlap, Kyle Mace, Julie Kipfer, Joe Josephson, and Hannah and Dale Sexton of Timber Trails for their support in supplying images for this book. A special appreciation also goes out to Terry Johnson for his critical last minute feedback and support.

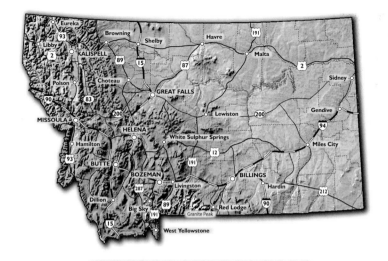

Acknowledgements

From Melynda:

A huge thanks, a warm hug and a cold beer to Mariann and Henry with whom I have toured many of the trails in this book with and who I have led onto trails that no cross-country skier should attempt. They both maintained high spirits in questionable circumstances. Of course, my number one ski partner was, and continues to be, Rigby who has shown me parts of the backcountry I would not have discovered on my own.

Thanks also to all the folks who have joined me on skiing adventures— Krista, Heather, Shelly, Andy, Angie, Julia, David, Greg, Woody, Becky, and their canine friends. Thanks to Jen for her help in proof-reading.

A big thanks to Joe Josephson who got us excited about this project again when we were almost ready to let it go.

From Mariann:

Joe Josephson for all his enthusiasm and for taking on this project when we had just about tucked it away on the shelf. I also would like to thank Rigby for motivating Melynda to don her skis on a regular basis and for providing so much entertainment during our excursions. I would not be a part of this book if it were not for Melynda – thanks for coming up with a great idea and seeing it through. No matter the destination or the snow conditions, our outings were, and still are, always full of laughter and a few good stories. Here's to many more powdery days and long, snow-filled winters. Cheers!

Beehive Basin near Big Sky.

CONTENTS

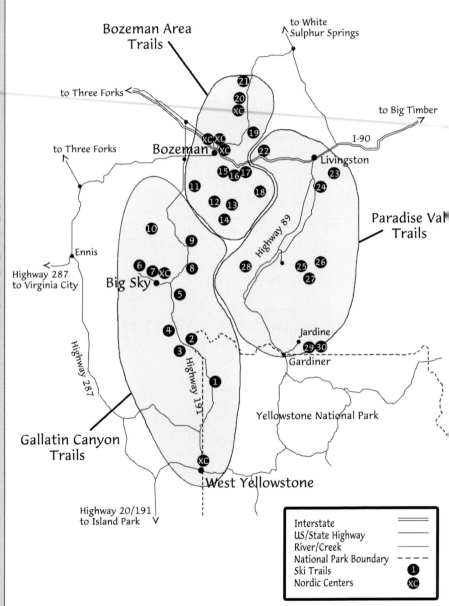

Bozeman Area Trails

to White Sulphur Springs

to Three Forks

to Big Timber

I-90

to Three Forks

Bozeman

Livingston

Paradise Valley Trails

Ennis

Highway 287 to Virginia City

Big Sky

Highway 89

Highway 287

Jardine

Gardiner

Gallatin Canyon Trails

Highway 191

Yellowstone National Park

Highway 20/191 to Island Park

West Yellowstone

Interstate	
US/State Highway	
River/Creek	
National Park Boundary	– – –
Ski Trails	❶
Nordic Centers	XC

Welcome to Winter in Southwest Montana

The idea for this book first came to me when I moved to Bozeman from Jackson, Wyoming. In Jackson I used a cross-country ski guide almost every winter day. It was my avenue into exploration of my temporary home.

When I moved to Bozeman I looked for a similar book that would get me started on ski touring the vast Forest Service lands in the area. Alas, there wasn't one. I decided to write a guide just as soon as I had figured out where the best ski tours were.

Those of us who live here, and those who visit, are fortunate to have a plethora of places to explore year-round. In the winter, frozen Passage Falls provides a spectacular turn around point on an already lovely tour. The open flats of Teepee Creek allow skiers to gaze into Yellowstone National Park and up at the surrounding peaks. Other trails, such as Bear Canyon or Bozeman Creek are social outings where families, friends, and dogs enjoy skiing close to home.

Six years and many ski tours later, I feel qualified to send others out onto the trails to kick and glide their way around the local mountains. Cross-country skiing is the way I get to spend time in the winter woods and meadows, get to recreate with friends, and get to wander around in my head while chickadees play background music and snow-laden boughs provide the scenery for my musings. I hope this book provides opportunities for others to do the same.

This book covers only 30 of the best and most popular trails in the southwest Montana portion of the Greater Yellowstone Ecosystem (GYE). This is but a fraction of the great tours here in our backyard. Yellowstone National Park is at the center of the GYE and surrounded by National Forest land. There are countless opportunities for skiers and snowshoers to explore the tall trees, rushing rivers, frozen falls, open vistas, craggy peaks and winter wildlife that fill this area.

In the near future, look for other cross-country ski guides from First Ascent Press including "Ski Trails of Yellowstone National Park & West Yellowstone" and "Ski Trails of Jackson Hole & Island Park" and eventually an expanded revision of this book with ski tours around Mammoth, Cooke City and elsewhere.

INTRODUCTION

Aprés Ski

After a long day in the snow—or sometimes in lieu of a day in the snow—nothing quite hits the spot like soaking in a hot spring or pouring back some suds. Here are just a few places to check out.

Paradise Valley

Boiling River (undeveloped)

A half-mile trail leads to a six-foot wide stream of hot water pouring over a travertine ledge into the Gardner River. Users have piled rocks to create a soaking area where the 140-degree water mixes with the cold river. Two miles south of Gardiner, MT near the 45th parallel sign in Yellowstone National Park, WY
(307) 344-7381 : www.nps.gov/yel/planyourvisit/nmammoth.htm

Chico Hot Springs Resort & Day Spa

This turn-of-the-century resort snuggled into the Absaroka Range features an outdoor swimming pool and an attached, covered soaking pool along with luxurious spa services. Chico Hot Springs resort is known for gourmet food—much of which is grown in the onsite garden and year round greenhouse—the Chico Bar is a local hot spot featuring great local bands.
#1 Old Chico Road, Pray, MT
1-800-468-9232 : www.chicohotsprings.com

Pine Creek Lodge & Café

Tucked into trees and not far from the Yellowstone River, the Pine Creek Café is a cozy and rustic restaurant that offers food, libations, music every Friday night and the popular "Winter Writer's Series" featuring readings by local, well-known authors.
2496 East River Road, Paradise Valley, MT : (406) 222-3628

The Night Spot Café

Tucked in behind other store fronts, The Night Spot is one of those secret haunts that is quickly gaining a reputation as one of the best restaurants in Livingston. If you are a carnivore, don't let the all-vegetarian fare turn you off the unique, flavorful dishes. Open until midnight, this charming café is the only non-fast food available in town after about 9:00 pm. Bring your own beer or wine.
113 West Park Street, Livingston, MT : (406) 222-4794

Bozeman

Bozeman Hot Springs

With a choice of nine pools including one outdoors, a dry sauna, the Amazon Rainforest room, a full service spa, a state-of-the-art fitness center, day care, and a juice bar, Bozeman Hot Springs is truly a family Mecca. If screaming kids aren't your thing, quickly head for the outdoor pool where it's a bit quieter.

81123 East Gallatin Road (US Highway 191), Four Corners, MT
(406) 586-6492 : www.bozemanhotspring.com

Bozeman Brewing Company

Although a relative newcomer, Bozeman Brewing Company (maker of Bozone Beers) is a local favorite. Since this is a tasting room, there is a three beer limit and it closes early, but it is the perfect spot for an *après* ski brew.

504 N. Broadway, Bozeman, MT
(406) 585-9142 : www.bozemanbrewing.com

The Garage

On a sunny day, there is nothing like sitting on the Garage patio sipping a well-deserved beer. The Garage also has indoor seating and serves great food, including the well-loved soup bar. Try the tomato-basil.

451 E. Main Street, Bozeman, MT : (406) 585-8558

Gallatin Canyon & Big Sky

Blue Moon Bakery

Stop here for a beer when you are anywhere near Big Sky, but the real gems are the baked goods. They also serve pizza, sandwiches and other fare. Everything is made from scratch and there is patio seating for nice days.

West Fork Meadows, Big Sky, MT : (406) 995-2305

The Corral Steakhouse

The Corral is a family steakhouse situated just down (south) the canyon from the Porcupine Creek Trail. It's old-school and has great burgers and fries—of course the beer isn't too bad either.

42895 Gallatin Road (US Highway 191)
Gallatin Canyon, MT : (406) 995-4249

Know Before You Go

Skis

Most of the tours in this book require nothing more than a light touring set-up. Local Nordic gear shops rent and sell the skis, boots and poles needed for a day of cross-country skiing.

I used a ski that is a little fatter than a track ski and has full metal edges to ski all the trails in this book. These skis provide more stability, the ability to sidestep and herringbone easily, and occasionally turn. They are also easier to snowplow into a stop than edgeless skis. Pair them with a mid-weight to sturdy boot and they can handle most touring conditions.

For steep terrain a telemark or randonee ski and boot are more appropriate. There are a few places in the "Taking it Further" section where they might be needed. But, realistically, a big backcountry set-up is unnecessary.

Waxless skis are convenient for all snow conditions and require little preparation. Basically, grab them and head out the door. From time to time, they'll need to be waxed and tuned, but for the most part they require little care.

Waxable skis are great for folks looking for higher performance, faster strides and more time spent trying to figure out which wax is the best for given conditions. For casually touring the trails in this book, stick to the waxless skis and carry some glide wax for sticky snow.

Clothes

Layers of synthetic fabric or wool—not cotton—are crucial to the cross-country skier. It's common to be quite warm and toasty while skiing and get very cold almost immediately after stopping. Add layers as soon as you feel chilled and remove layers as soon as you warm up.

A breathable hat, long underwear (or ski tights), and socks make a decent base layer. Depending on the weather, add cross-country ski pants, a mid-weight shirt, jacket and gloves. Gaiters will keep the snow out of boots and pants.

Food & Water

Internal heat production is dependent on nutrition and calories. Take enough food and water for the amount of time you plan to be out, plus a little more, just in case. Stop to eat and drink frequently throughout the day, rather than taking one or two breaks and consuming a lot of food.

Water is especially important. Winter air is cold and dry, so every time you take a breath in, the air has to be warmed by your body. Your exhalation is moisture-laden and that water needs to be replaced to prevent dehydration. Combine that with heavy breathing from exertion and the average person is losing a lot more water out skiing than sitting around the house.

Water can be heated in the morning, poured into a water bottle, wrapped in an extra layer of clothing and nestled into a backpack to keep it from freezing. Or, invest in a good thermos and enjoy a warm beverage all day long. Be sure to bring enough for your skiing partners—they'll be coveting your hot drink.

Other Equipment

It's always a good idea to carry a map and compass or Global Positioning System (GPS). Sudden snow storms can make it impossible to see your route, or even follow your ski tracks back to the car.

The most important piece of equipment to bring is a buddy. Winter recreation can be dangerous; it is a good idea to have someone with you if things should go wrong. And let someone at home know where you are going and when you plan to be back.

Avalanches

If traveling in avalanche terrain a transceiver, shovel and probe pole—and the knowledge of how to use them—are mandatory. Most tours in this book avoid avalanche terrain, but if venturing off the trail, be sure to know what you are doing.

The Gallatin National Forest Avalanche Center offers both basic and advanced avalanche classes throughout the winter. These classes are a good way for anyone spending time outside in the winter to become more "avalanche aware". The website also includes an avalanche advisory, weather conditions and other pertinent information. For a calendar of classes or other info visit *www.mtavalanche.com*.

Winter Safety

There are a host of possible injuries and ailments that winter recreationalists need to consider. This is not a book on winter first aid or safety, but here are a few things to consider to make your trip as safe as possible.

- As mentioned above, ski with at least one other person.
- Let someone know where you are skiing.
- Know your abilities and stick to routes appropriate to your level of skiing. If a trail turns out to be more difficult than expected, turn around and choose another tour. (Or sit in a hot spring with this book and plan your next outing.)

AVALANCHE AWARENESS

Check the weather and avalanche forecast before you head out into the snow. For avalanche conditions on the Gallatin National Forest visit *www.mtavalanche.com* or call the *Avalanche Hotline at (406) 587-6981*.

FROSTBITE

Recognize the warning signs and know how to treat frostbite and hypothermia. Below are just a few points on frostbite and hypothermia, take a first aid class and learn for yourself how to handle winter emergencies.

- Frostbite is literally frozen body tissue. Hands and feet usually get frostbitten first as blood vessels constrict to route blood (and warmth) to the body's core.
- Children are more at risk of getting frostbite because they lose heat faster than adults. Children may also be less willing to give up their winter fun time, so watch kids carefully.

Frostbite symptoms include:

- Discoloration of skin (white, waxy or purplish), skin may darken after a few hours if left untreated
- Skin may feel rock hard
- Burning or tingling feeling
- Partial or complete numbness
- Possibly intense pain

To treat frostbite, get inside as quickly as possible. Remove wet clothes and place affected body part in warm (not hot) water. Seek medical attention.

If it is impossible to get inside, remove wet clothing and replace with dry layers. Increase physical activity to warm up and to get back to your vehicle quickly.

HYPOTHERMIA

Hypothermia is when the temperature of the body drops below the level required for normal metabolism. Again, children are more susceptible than adults due to their small body size and high surface-to-volume ratio. An important point to remember is that it doesn't have to be very cold for someone to become hypothermic.

Hypothermia symptoms include:

* Mild shivering that becomes more violent (and eventually stops followed by a sense that you are warm)
* Tiredness, lethargy or a reluctance to keep moving
* Confusion, fumbling, poor decision making
* Face, fingers and toes may become pale or blue as heat is sucked to the body's core
* Collapsing

To treat hypothermia remove wet clothes and replace them with warm, dry layers. If the victim is conscious, have them drink a warm beverage (never alcohol!). Keep the victim moving as much as possible and try to get back to your vehicle.

If the victim cannot move, seek shelter out of the wind. Replace wet clothes with dry, warm layers, keep the victim still and horizontal and use your own body heat to warm them while someone else gets help.

Of course, it is better to avoid either of these situations than to treat them. Dress appropriately, check the weather forecast, carry extra food, water and clothing, and don't get into situations that are beyond your ability.

Trail Etiquette

On National Forest lands (where the vast majority of trails in this book are located) almost anything goes. Likely, the cross-country skier will encounter families, dogs, snowshoers, snowmobilers and others while enjoying a day in the snow. To keep everyone happy, consider the following rules of etiquette:

- Don't walk or snowshoe in ski tracks if at all possible.
- Many of us love to bring our canine friend along on winter adventures, and they are welcome on National Forest lands. Make sure yours doesn't bother other people or chase wildlife. Keep dogs under verbal control or use a leash if necessary.
- Remove poop from the trail—no one wants to ski through it.
- Yield to downhill skiers.
- Step off the trail for breaks or to chat.
- If you fall and make a big hole in the trail, fill it in.
- If you need to poop, the best option is to simply go before you get on the trail. If you absolutely must go, the most environmentally sound option is to pack it out. If you dig a hole in the snow, it will just stay frozen until the snow melts and then be left sitting on the ground. Don't worry, it doesn't have to be gross to carry your poop out. Use any one of the excellent WagBag® or Rest Stop® products. www.whennaturecalls.com
- Pee away from the trail and cover the yellow snow so no one else has to look at it.

Photo © Mariann Van Den Elzen.

Gallatin National Forest Travel Management Plan

In December 2006 the Gallatin National Forest Service published a new travel plan for the entire Forest that describes what kind of uses are allowed and where. In general, the winter aspects of this management plan make more land accessible and available to cross-country skiers. However, the plan is being contested by several other user groups and thus may be tied up in court for awhile.

Not knowing what the future holds for a handful of key areas, this book leaves out some trails that might become great cross-country ski tours (specifically tours in the Hyalite area and Rock Creek on the east side of the Gallatin Range). Visit www.firstascentpress. com or contact any of the Forest Service offices to find out about some great new areas that may be appropriate for cross-country skiing in the near future.

Gallatin National Forest
www.fs.fed.us/r1/gallatin/

Bozeman Ranger District
(406) 522-2520

Livingston Ranger District
(406) 222-1892

Gardiner Office
(406) 848-7375

Forest Service Cabins

Forest Service cabins are a great way to extend a cross-country ski tour. Overnighting at one of the 23 cabins on the Gallatin National Forest provides the feeling of being out in the backcountry while enjoying many of the comforts of home. Plus, with a lighter backpack than if you were winter camping—no need to carry a stove, sleeping pad or other camping necessities—it's easy to go light and cover more miles, or to bring in gourmet food and libations to fill those long winter nights.

All cabins have wood stoves and wood, and many have propane lanterns; some have electricity, but none have water in the winter. Visit www.fs.fed.us/r1/gallatin/ to find out more about these great cabins or to reserve a space.

Nordic Centers & Groomed Ski Areas

The trails covered in this book are front and backcountry trails, but there are plenty of local Nordic Centers for those days you'd prefer skiing on corduroy, want to skate ski or only have a limited amount of time. Dogs are not allowed on these ski trails, except at the Snowfill site and Hyalite.

Bozeman

Bohart Ranch Cross Country Ski Center

27+ kilometers of superb groomed ski trails are situated on private and Forest Service lands and loop through terrain well suited to all ability levels. The Kiddy Kilometer Trail is a signed interpretative trail popular with families and younger skiers. They also feature snowshoe trails. 16 miles northeast of Bozeman near Bridger Bowl. *www.bohartranchxcski.com*

Bridger Creek Golf Course

The golf course trails provide skiing right in town. The golf course is groomed by the Bridger Ski Foundation (BSF) and operates on donations. Buy a button at the ski trails or at local shops.

Lindley Park

Groomed by the BSF and supported through button sales and donations, these trails, near the Hospital, loop through agricultural fields and provide excellent skiing right in town. *www.bsfnordic.com*

Snowfill Site

Snowfill is an experiment in progress and open to skiers with dogs. It is currently groomed by a hard working volunteer, but things may change in the future as the City of Bozeman builds a summer park.

Bridger Creek Golf Course
Photo © Bob Allen Photography.

In addition to the above groomed ski trails, the City of Bozeman and the BSF are looking at grooming some additional fifty miles of trail within and around Bozeman. Visit **www.bsfnordic.com** for updates.

Email bridgernordic@bresnan.net to be added to the mailing list and kept up to date on the grooming schedules for all Bozeman groomed areas and Golf Courses.

Hyalite Canyon

This unique canyon, south of Bozeman, is one of the most-heavily recreated areas in the state and is home to some of the best cross-country ski terrain in the county. A few well-established tours in Hyalite are described here in detail, however, many more groomed loops are under improvement by the BSF; led primarily by long time Hyalite XC ski advocate Terry Johnson.

The pace of this development is dictated not only by the sheer hard work involved but also by a staged process where the BSF is working closely with the Southwest Montana Climbers Coalition (ice climbers), the Gallatin National Forest and other users to progressively manage use of the Hyalite Road in light of the recent decisions regarding the Travel Management Plan. Stay tuned. *www.hyalite.org*

Big Sky

Lone Mountain Ranch

Dry, Rocky Mountain snow covers 80 kilometers of groomed trails. Yellow Mountain fills most of the view to the north of the trail system and is home to big horn sheep and other wildlife. Many of the upper trails provide a great workout with their steep climbs and quick descents. *www.lonemountainranch.com*

West Yellowstone

Rendezvous Ski Trails

35 kilometers of gently rolling, beautifully groomed trails that wind through tall stands of lodgepole pine and open meadows. West Yellowstone often has more snow than the Bozeman area, so Rendezvous Ski Trails are ideal for early and late season skiing. *www.rendezvousskitrails.com*

Photo © Mariann Van Den Elzen.

Got Gear?

No great ski region would be complete without the quality outdoor specialty stores that serve as local nerve centers for ski trail conditions, updates on new trails, wax and other supplies, equipment rentals, gear and apparel sales.

Livingston

Timber Trails

309 W. Park, (406) 222-9550

Bozeman

Northern Lights Trading Co.

1716 W. Babcock, (406) 586-2225

www.northernlightstrading.com

Bangtail Bikes and Ski

508 W. Main, (406) 587-4905

www.bangtailbikes.com

Big Sky

Grizzly Outfitters

11 Lone Peak Drive, (406) 995-2939

www.grizzlyoutfitters.com

Lone Mountain Ranch

1 Lone Mountain Ranch Rd, (406) 995-4734

www.lmranch.com

West Yellowstone

Free Heel & Wheel

40 Yellowstone Ave, (406) 646-7744

www.freeheelandwheel.com

How to Use This Book

Each of the tours in this book has been both researched and skied by the author. Standard information is listed for every tour that should help you determine whether or not you want to ski it. Additionally, each tour is accompanied by a trail map and elevation profile for a better visual representation.

The categories listed for every trail are:

Distance: The horizontal mileage of the tour as obtained from topographic maps. It is noted whether the mileage is "round trip" (out and back) or for a "loop" trail.

Elevation Gain: The distance in elevation the tour climbs, measured in feet. Trails may climb and descend many times between the start and the turn around point; this number indicates the total elevation gained on the trail.

Maps: While this book provides accurate maps, some trails—or some users—may require more detailed maps that show topography or more detail. Listed are the specific USGS topographical maps that cover the tours and a larger, regional map created by Beartooth Publishing.

Trail Report: A brief synopsis of what the terrain and scenery of the trail look like. The Trail Report may also include other types of users that often utilize the trail or other pertinent information.

Getting There: Driving directions to the trailhead from the nearest town.

Skiing: Specific directions for skiing the tour. Used in combination with the accompanying map, these skiing directions should provide ample information to prepare for your tour.

With Kids: Whether the tour is appropriate for kids.

Disclaimer

This book is a general reference guide only and does not take the place of your own skiing ability, route-finding capacity or judgment.

Many of the tours also include the following:

Taking it Further: Brief overview of what other skiing options are available from a given trailhead. Skiers wishing to further explore an area should get more detailed maps and research the route for themselves. The "Taking it Further" section may contain routes in avalanche-prone areas and skiers must know how to identify possible avalanche risks, what equipment is needed and how to use it, and what to do if involved in an avalanche incident.

Snowshoeing: Synopsis of snowshoeing opportunities from the trailhead or other points on the tour.

Nature Notes: Interesting facts and information about ecology, species or other natural history topics likely to be encountered on a given trail.

History Hints: Human history related to a specific tour.

Noteworthy Views: All the tours in this book are scenic, but some have more spectacular views than others or just something unique to that area. This section notes what to look for.

Maps:

Each tour (or tours) has an accompanying map. These maps help the skier chart where they are going. In whiteout or poor weather conditions, a map may not be enough and a compass or GPS unit may also be needed along with the skill and ability to use them.

Reading the Map—the Legend:

Reading the Map—the Elevation Profile:

The elevation profile is a cutaway diagram that shows level land, hills, and steeper mountains. Example:

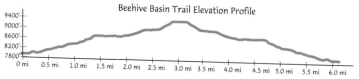

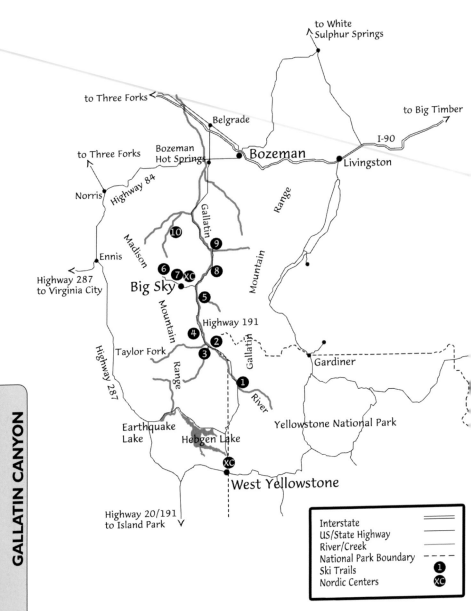

GALLATIN CANYON

The Big Sky area and Gallatin Canyon are highly scenic (parts of *A River Runs Through It* were filmed here) as are the tours in this section. Trails head into both the Gallatin Range on the east side of the canyon and the Madison Range on the west side.

The Gallatin River originates in Gallatin Lake, below Three Rivers Peak in Yellowstone National Park. It parallels Crowfoot Ridge while gurgling and purling through alpine meadows before merging with Grayling Creek and becoming wedged into Gallatin Canyon.

The river, the canyon, the lake and the mountain range were all named for Albert Gallatin, President Jefferson's Secretary of Treasury from 1801-1814. When Lewis and Clark came through Montana on their way to the Pacific in 1905, they named the three rivers that form the Missouri the Jefferson, the Madison and the Gallatin (it's always a good idea to keep your patrons happy by naming things after them). They followed the Jefferson River thinking (correctly) it would lead most directly to the mountains separating them from the big ocean.

The Madison River, after which the mountains were named, flows on the other side of the Madison Range.

The Gallatin Canyon tours range from wide open valleys—such as Tepee Creek—to tight, treed trails like Cinnamon Mountain. Whichever trails you choose, you are sure to be in for a delightful tour in some of the most beautiful places in the country.

Photo © Mariann Van Den Elzen.
Gallatin Canyon.

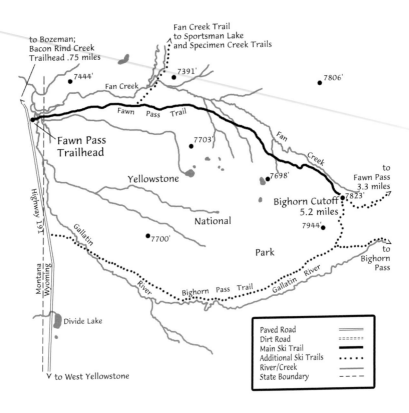

Fawn Pass Trail Elevation Profile

GALLATIN CANYON

1 : Fawn Pass Trail

Distance: 10.4 miles round trip

Elevation Gain: 695 feet

Topo Maps: USGS: Divide Lake, Joseph Peak, Quadrant, Mammoth
Beartooth Publishing: "Bozeman, Big Sky to West"

Trail Report: The *crème de le crème* of cross-country skiing near Big Sky, Fawn Pass is loved by skate skiers, telemarkers and snowshoers as well as those donning classic cross-country gear. There are various touring opportunities, all in Yellowstone National Park, so leave your dog at home for this outing.

Getting There: From Bozeman take Huffine Lane west 6 miles to Four Corners. Turn left (south) on Highway 191 and continue 56.8 miles (25.8 miles past the turnoff to Big Sky) to the signed trail on the left. Look for a big pull out just south of milepost 22.

Skiing: From the trailhead ski east up a big open valley crossing several fingers of the Gallatin River. Narrow snow bridges and logs cross the waterways, but you may need to remove your skis for some crossings.

At 1.3 miles go straight at the intersection with the Fan Creek Trail. The trail climbs a little more steeply just before the junction with the Bighorn Pass Cutoff Trail at 5.2 miles. This is a good turn around spot; the trail gets steeper from here on out.

With Kids: The lower part of the trail is gently inclining, and a good bet for young skiers.

Taking it Further: So many options! The Fan Creek Trail (1.3 miles from the trailhead) heads northeast following Fan Creek. This trail is relatively mellow all the way to the junction with the Sportsman Lake Trail. Turning left (northwest) at that junction will take you to the Specimen Creek Trail and back to Highway 191. It's a big, big loop.

At the Bighorn Pass Cutoff Trail (5.2 miles from the trailhead) it is possible to head south, then west on the Bighorn Pass Trail to make a big loop. Again, you'll be dumped out on Highway 191, this time south of your vehicle. For this you may want to arrange another car to leave at the Bighorn parking area to complete this superb outing.

1 : Fawn Pass

For those continuing to Fawn Pass, ski straight ahead at the Big Horn Pass Cutoff Trail. The trail climbs through intermittently burned forests and big, open meadows to Fawn Pass at 8.5 miles. Fawn Pass isn't a sharp divide like many passes, but rather a gently rolling hill. Have a picnic, enjoy the views and then head back the way you came. Fawn Pass is popular with telemark skiers, so if you have tele skis and are heading to Fawn Pass anyway, might as well ditch the classic set-up and strap on the teles.

Or, continue past Fawn Pass all the way to the Glen Creek Trailhead, south of Mammoth Hot Springs. You'll need backcountry techniques, fortitude and a car shuttle to complete this 20.8 mile through-ski.

The Fawn Pass area is also popular with skate skiers. In spring, the snow warms up during the day and re-freezes at night, creating a perfect "crust-cruising" surface, at least until it heats up in the late morning. Skate skiers practically fly across the valley when the conditions are right. No need to follow a trail; instead follow your whimsy.

Snowshoeing: Snowshoeing up Fawn Pass is OK, but you'll wish you had your skis. Instead, cross the highway from the trailhead and head up Bacon Rind Creek Drainage. There is a trail, but a better snowshoe adventure can be had by blazing your own path.

Nature Notes: This scenic area is prime moose habitat; watch for moose especially in the brush along the streams. Also, keep an eye open for elk, deer, snowshoe hares and a plethora of other wildlife.

Just beyond the Bighorn Creek Cutoff Trail is where the Gallatin Range bear management area starts. Of course, in the middle of winter there are unlikely to be bears around, but if you are skiing in spring, keep an alert look out for Griz.

GALLATIN CANYON

Skate skiing on the spring crust near the Fawn Pass Trail.
Photo © Bob Allen Photography.

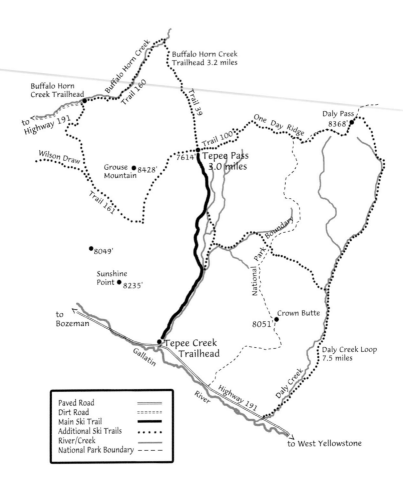

Buffalo Horn Creek Trailhead 3.2 miles

Buffalo Horn Creek Trailhead

to Highway 191

Trail 160

Buffalo Horn Creek

Trail 39

Daly Pass 8368'

One Day Ridge

Trail 100

7614' Tepee Pass 3.0 miles

Wilson Draw

Grouse Mountain ● 8428'

Trail 161

● 8049'

Sunshine Point ● 8235'

National Park Boundary

Crown Butte
8051'

to Bozeman

Tepee Creek Trailhead

Gallatin

River

Highway 191

Daly Creek

Daly Creek Loop 7.5 miles

to West Yellowstone

Paved Road	═══
Dirt Road	═══
Main Ski Trail	▬▬▬
Additional Ski Trails	• • • •
River/Creek	▬▬▬
National Park Boundary	– – –

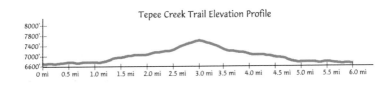

Tepee Creek Trail Elevation Profile

8000'
7800'
7400'
7000'
6600'

0 mi 0.5 mi 1.0 mi 1.5 mi 2.0 mi 2.5 mi 3.0 mi 3.5 mi 4.0 mi 4.5 mi 5.0 mi 5.5 mi 6.0 mi

2 : Tepee Creek Trail

Distance: 6 miles round trip

Elevation Gain: 950 feet

Topo Maps: USGS: Sunshine Point
Beartooth Publishing: "Bozeman, Big Sky to West"

Trail Report: This trail follows Tepee Creek through a sage-spotted landscape. Lodgepole pines dot the wide valley and cover the hills. Yellowstone National Park is just south and can be accessed from this trail, but dogs are not allowed in the Park.

Getting There: From Bozeman take Huffine Lane west 6 miles to Four Corners. Turn left (south) on Highway 191 and continue 49.8 miles (16 miles past the turnoff to Big Sky) to the signed trail on the left. Look for the Forest Service sign and park 100 yards up the dirt access road.

Skiing: From the trailhead ski up the wide valley following Tepee Creek. After 1.1 miles, arrive at a Forest Service sign.

Take the left trail and ski towards Buffalo Horn Divide. After 2 miles, and lots of gently rolling ups and downs, you reach Tepee Pass and a signed junction. About 200 yards up the right (east) trail is a flat area with viewing opportunities.

Our tour ends at Tepee Pass—head back the same route as the ascent.

With Kids: Tepee Pass is an easy ski and perfect for kids. Gentle hills on either side of the creek are perfect for practicing downhill skills and general messing around.

Taking it Further: At the Forest Service sign at 1.1 miles the trail to the right heads over the divide, into Yellowstone National Park and meets up with the Daly Creek Trail. This 7.5 mile loop encircles Crown Butte and necessitates an off-trail ski between the two trailheads. Dogs are not allowed on the trails in Yellowstone.

At Tepee Pass, the right (east) trail leads to One Day Ridge and Daly Pass, then drops down to Daly Creek.

To the left (west), the trail traverses Grouse Mountain as it heads into Wilson Draw and to the Gallatin River. The trail straight ahead (north) descends 1.8 miles to Buffalo Horn Creek Trail. It's another 1.4 miles to the Buffalo Horn trailhead.

Snowshoeing: Tepee Creek Trail is an easy snowshoe. Head up one of the many sidehills to pick up your heart rate and alter the route and view.

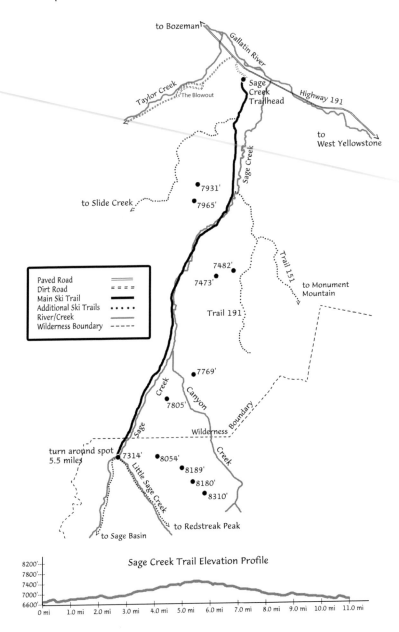

Sage Creek Trail Elevation Profile

3 : Sage Creek Trail

Distance: up to 11 miles round trip

Elevation Gain: 665 feet

Topo Maps: USGS: Sunshine Point & Upper Tepee Basin
Beartooth Publishing: "Bozeman, Big Sky to West"

Trail Report: Sage Creek Trail starts in open sagebrush, moves into the trees and travels through the Lee Metcalf Wilderness to Sage Basin, all the while following Sage Creek. This out-and-back ski can be made just about any length. Ski until you don't feel like it anymore and then turn around.

Getting There: From Bozeman take Huffine Lane west 6 miles to Four Corners. Turn left (south) on Highway 191 and continue 48 miles (14.2 miles past the turnoff to Big Sky). Just past the Taylor Fork Road is another road. Turn right. Drive 0.4 miles to the end of the access road.

Skiing: Ski south from the parking area 0.5 miles to the first trail junction. Veer left. The trail to the right is Slide Creek and a much steeper ascent. At 1.75 miles there is another trail junction where the trail first meets the creek. This time ski to the right.

The trail continues to climb gradually, with various little ups and downs along the way and crossing the creek several times. At 5.5 miles you'll come to another trail junction, less than 0.5 miles after entering the Wilderness Area. This is our turn around spot.

With Kids: This might be suitable for kids who ski well and can turn and stop effectively. Otherwise, there are better options for kid-skiing.

Taking it Further: At the turn around spot, the right (east) trail continues up Sage Creek 5.7 miles to Sage Basin. Here it connects with several other trails.

The left (west) trail follows Little Sage Creek another 3 miles to a large cirque surrounded by Sage Peak (10,664), Redstreak Peak (10,384) and Cone Peak (9,678).

Snowshoeing: This can be a nice trail to snowshoe. Try exploring some of the steeper side trails for a little more adventure.

3 : Sage Creek

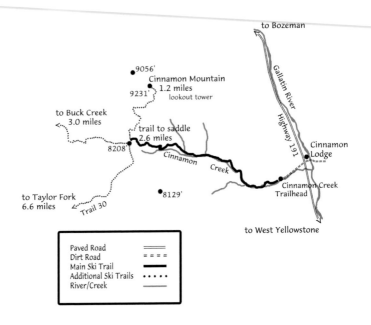

9056'

Cinnamon Mountain
1.2 miles
lookout tower

9231'

to Buck Creek
3.0 miles

trail to saddle
2.6 miles

8208'

Cinnamon Creek

to Taylor Fork
6.6 miles

Trail 30

8129'

Gallatin River

Highway 191

Cinnamon Lodge

Cinnamon Creek Trailhead

to Bozeman

to West Yellowstone

Paved Road	════
Dirt Road	= = = =
Main Ski Trail	▬▬▬
Additional Ski Trails	• • • • •
River/Creek	───

GALLATIN CANYON

Cinnamon Creek Trail Elevation Profile

8500'
8000'
7500'
7000'
6500'

0 mi   0.5 mi   1.0 mi   1.5 mi   2.0 mi   2.5 mi   3.0 mi   3.5 mi   4.0 mi   4.5 mi   5.0 mi   5.5 mi

4 : Cinnamon Creek Trail

Distance: 5.2 miles round trip

Elevation Gain: 1,640 feet

Topo Maps: USGS: Lincoln Mountain & Sunshine Point
Beartooth Publishing: "Bozeman, Big Sky to West"

Trail Report: You'll see the lookout tower on Cinnamon Mountain as you drive down the Gallatin Valley toward the trailhead. The trail skirts below the southern flank of the mountain.

Getting There: From Bozeman take Huffine Lane west 6 miles to Four Corners. Turn left (south) on Highway 191 and continue 44.7 miles (10.9 miles past the turnoff to Big Sky). Turn right just past the Cinnamon Lodge and gas station and drive 0.37 miles to the end of the road.

Skiing: From the trailhead, ski west along Cinnamon Creek, crossing the creek several times as you steadily climb. This trail is a little on the steep side for cross-country skis, but doable with a little focus and skill.

At 0.75 miles ascend a switchback with another one not too far ahead. A little beyond the 1.5 mark, the trail leaves the creek, joining it briefly again at 2.1 miles and then climbing away from the water for the last 0.5 miles to the saddle.

The saddle is our turn around spot. The ski down from the saddle will be quick, practice your half wedge and don't be afraid to sit down if you get out of control!

With Kids: There are better places to ski with kids.

Taking it Further: From the saddle, the trail to the right (north) climbs steeply to the top of Cinnamon Mountain (9,235 feet). The trail to the left (south) winds around and eventually connects with the Taylor Fork Road. The trail continuing straight ahead meets up with some logging roads, and then Buck Creek.

Snowshoeing: This is a nice trail to snowshoe, it may be better for snowshoeing than skiing and it is easier to get to the lookout tower on snowshoes than skis.

4 : Cinnamon Creek

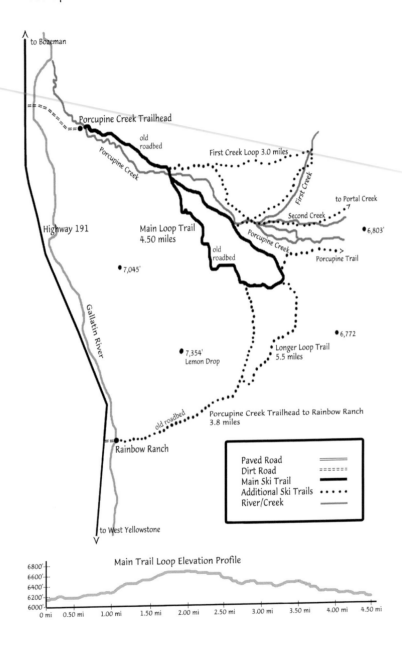

to Bozeman

Porcupine Creek Trailhead

old roadbed

Porcupine Creek

First Creek Loop 3.0 miles

First Creek

Highway 191

to Portal Creek

Second Creek

● 6,803'

Main Loop Trail
4.50 miles

Porcupine Creek

old roadbed

Porcupine Trail

● 7,045'

● 6,772

Gallatin River

● 7,354'
Lemon Drop

Longer Loop Trail
5.5 miles

old roadbed

Porcupine Creek Trailhead to Rainbow Ranch
3.8 miles

Rainbow Ranch

Paved Road	─────
Dirt Road	═══════
Main Ski Trail	━━━━
Additional Ski Trails	• • • •
River/Creek	─────

to West Yellowstone

Main Trail Loop Elevation Profile

6800'
6600'
6400'
6200'
6000'
0 mi   0.50 mi   1.00 mi   1.50 mi   2.00 mi   2.50 mi   3.00 mi   3.50 mi   4.00 mi   4.50 mi

GALLATIN CANYON

5 : Porcupine Creek Trail

Distance: 4.5 to 5 miles round trip (lollipop loop)

Elevation Gain: 560 feet

Topo Maps: USGS: Lone Indian Peak
Beartooth Publishing: "Bozeman, Big Sky to West"

Trail Report: There are many trail and loop options on the Porcupine Creek Trail. This tour makes a loop with extended views into the Gallatin Range and time near the creek. Snowmobiles are prohibited in this drainage, as it is part of the Porcupine Elk Reserve—winter range for Rocky Mountain elk.

Getting There: From Bozeman take Huffine Lane west 6 miles to Four Corners. Turn left (south) on Highway 191 and continue 36.5 miles to Porcupine Creek Road on the left (2.7 miles past the Big Sky turnoff). Drive .5 miles (or as far as passable) to the end of the road and the trailhead sign.

Skiing: Ski along the trail just beyond the trailhead sign, through the gate, past a cabin and across a bridge. Passing a trail on the left, continue to the right on the main trail. The route is pretty flat and parallels the creek to the second bridge at 1 mile. Cross the bridge over Porcupine

Porcupine Creek.
Photo © Mariann Van Den Elzen.

Creek and keep to the right on the old roadbed. Ignore the trail to the left immediately after the bridge with the small trail marker.

Head up the hill on the roadbed, catching views of several Gallatin peaks. As the roadbed winds around, it crosses big, open hills and affords views up the Porcupine Drainage—one of the prettiest sites in the Gallatins with the high peaks in the background.

The roadbed eventually hooks up with the Porcupine Creek Trail in the valley at 2.9 miles, but there are several fun places to head down and create your own trail to the creek. Upon meeting the main trail, head west 1.5-2 miles (depending on where you meet it) to the trailhead.

With Kids: The first mile of this trail is great for kids; it is relatively flat and wide and ends at a bridge over Porcupine Creek.

Taking it Further: There are lots of options for longer tours in the Porcupine Creek valley. Instead of leaving the roadbed and joining the Porcupine Creek Trail, stay on the road while it winds around to Rainbow Ranch. Leave a car here for a shuttle back to the trailhead.

Another option is to turn right (east) at the junction of the roadbed and the Porcupine Creek Trail. This route heads up the drainage.

Yet another option is to stay left at the second creek crossing and ski towards First Creek. Just after crossing First Creek, head right (south) to meet back up with the Porcupine Creek Trail.

Snowshoeing: This area is wide open and ideal for the snowshoer who likes to explore. Stick to one of the many trails in the area or head off on your own to break new trail.

Nature Notes: Moose often congregate in the willows just off the highway. Moose have articulated knees so they can lift their legs straight out of the snow. Other animals, like elk and deer, cannot bend their knees in the same way and instead must plow through the snow, therefore expending a lot more energy.

Noteworthy Views: From the roadbed and higher up, one gains a great vantage point to view Eaglehead Mountain (9,979 feet) and the Gallatin Crest.

GALLATIN CANYON

Elk (Cervus canadensis)

One of the most majestic animals in the Greater Yellowstone Ecosystem is the elk, aka Wapiti. The males sport large antlers (antlers fall off each year, whereas horns don't) atop their reddish brown bodies. A yellow rump patch helps identify them from a distance.

Male elk can be as big as a large horse, 600-800 pounds; females tend to range from 500-525 pounds. Only the males grow antlers, which on a mature bull can have six to eight tines on each side and weigh 30 pounds.

Twenty to twenty-five thousand elk spend the summer in Yellowstone National Park, but due to heavy snow in the winter—and thus not much available food—most of those elk winter at lower elevations. The Porcupine Creek drainage is another place elk congregate in the winter, so the Forest Service has protected this area for them.

Elk are famous for their mating call, known as a "bugle". During mating season, individual male elk gather as many females as they can (20-30) into a harem. Then they have to protect them from other males, often fighting, locking antlers, and occasionally dieing.

The elk's bugle starts with low, stirring, clear notes and rises to a high-pitched shrill. Unfortunately, winter visitors won't hear any bugling since it takes place during the rut, or mating season (September-early October).

During the day elk usually hang out in conifer forests, but if you are an early riser—or late skier—you may catch a glimpse of them in the meadows at dawn and dusk.

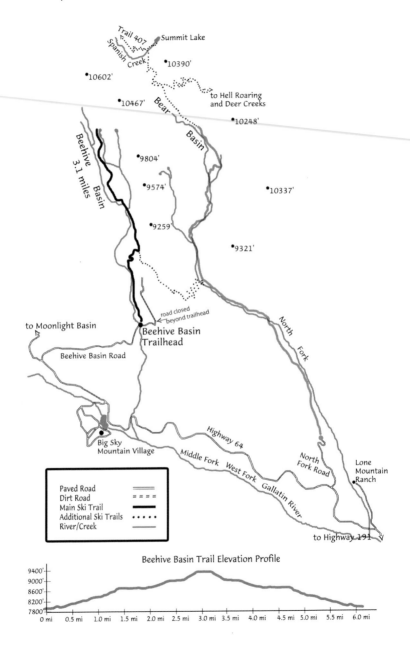

Beehive Basin Trail Elevation Profile

6 : Beehive Basin Trail

Distance: 6.2 miles round trip

Elevation Gain: 1,364 feet

Topo Maps: USGS: Lone Mountain
Beartooth Publishing: "Bozeman, Big Sky to West"

Trail Report: The Beehive Basin Trail makes for a nice, mellow cross-country tour interspersed with climbs up a series of benches. It is also very popular with backcountry skiers. If you prefer making turns to kicking and gliding, this is the trail for you. See photo on Contents page.

Getting There: From Bozeman take Huffine Lane west 6 miles to Four Corners. Turn left (south) on Highway 191 and continue 33.8 miles to the Big Sky turnoff. Turn right (west) and follow the road 10 miles to the Beehive Basin turnoff on the right, just before reaching Moonlight Basin. Drive up the gravel road 1.6 miles to the trailhead. Park on the left side of the road.

Beehive Basin.
Photo © Julie Kipfer.

Skiing: From the parking area, ski up the trail, probably following others' tracks. On the ridge above sit million dollar houses, making for a surreal wilderness experience. They peter out quickly.

Right away you'll cross a stream. The trail follows the valley through a large meadow and then ascends to another meadow and a pond.

Climb a little further and the trail flattens out at an unnamed lake (frozen and covered with snow) and a cirque at 3.1 miles. Enjoy the spectacular views before descending the same way you came.

With Kids: Some older kids might like this ski and appreciate the alpine setting. The descent may be tricky for younger children.

Snowshoeing: This is an ideal place for snowshoeing. It is easy to follow skiers' trails without actually walking on them. Additionally, opportunities abound for exploring. Watch for avalanche danger above the cirque.

Taking it Further: For backcountry skiers, there are plenty of nice lines above the cirque. Some skiers prefer to climb the ridge to the right near the start of the trail and follow it up to the cirque, rather than skiing up the valley.

Nature Notes: At the top of the climb to the second meadow and pond you are crossing a fault line, moving from sedimentary limestone onto igneous gneiss. If you follow the fault to the walls of the basin you'll notice the easily eroded limestone up against the black and white striped gneiss.

Noteworthy Views: On the ski up, you'll be graced with views of 10,335 ft Blaze Mountain; 11,015 ft Gallatin Peak is just to the east of the Blaze. Skiing down, enjoy views of Lone Mountain and beautiful Fan Mountain.

Lone Mountain

What else is there to do in Big Sky?

Big Sky is an interesting little community spread throughout an especially scenic valley. There isn't really a "downtown" Big Sky, but rather several small shopping and business centers. If you've had enough cross-country skiing in the spectacular backcountry of the Madison Range, here are some other things to do:

Downhill Ski

Switch into your alpine skis or telemark gear and head downhill at one of Big Sky's ski areas—Big Sky Resort or Moonlight Basin. Combined, they are the largest ski resort in America. Both ski areas are located on Lone Peak and you can even buy a pass that allows access to both resorts. www.bigskyresort.com, www.moonlightbasin.com

Take a Hike

Even in winter, it's possible to walk down the paved path to Ousel Falls. This cascading 35 ft fall is located behind Meadow Village on the Ousel Falls Road. Follow Route 64 (Spur Road) into Big Sky. After passing the Meadow Golf Course on your right, turn left onto Ousel Falls Road. Continue on this road for a little over 2 miles until you see the Ousel Falls Park and Yellow Mules Trail sign on your left. Park here; access to the trail is well marked. From the parking area, a wide path leads one way to the waterfall and in the other direction into Big Sky.

Cross-Country Ski on Corduroy

Big Sky is home to a beautiful Nordic center—Lone Mountain Ranch. You don't have to be a guest at the ranch to use the 80 km of ski trails—groomed for both striding and skating. Lone Mountain Ranch offers a Professional Ski Instructors of America (PSIA) certified ski school, as well as rental and retail equipment. You can also sign up for a guided ski or snowshoe tour in nearby Yellowstone National Park.

Lone Mountain's trails are fairly hilly, but there are some mellow trails down low and a dog loop (known locally as the "poop loop"). And even though it is a groomed area, most of the trails feel secluded and wild. www.lmranch.com

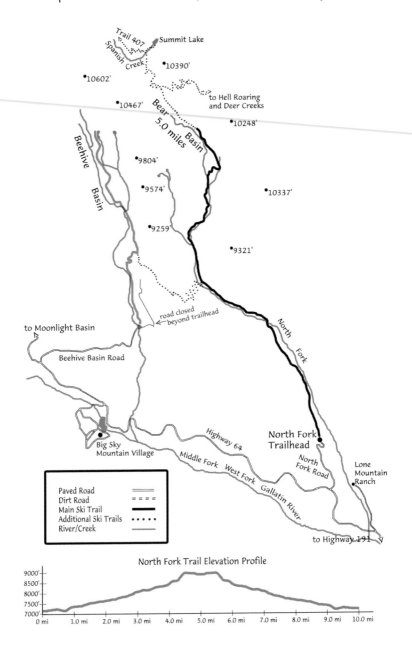

Trail 407
Summit Lake
Spanish Creek
•10390'
•10602'
•10467'
Bear Basin
5.0 miles
to Hell Roaring
and Deer Creeks
•10248'
•9804'
•10337'
•9574'
•9259'
•9321'
Beehive Basin

road closed
beyond trailhead

to Moonlight Basin

Beehive Basin Road

North Fork

North Fork
Trailhead

Big Sky
Mountain Village

Highway 64

Middle Fork   West Fork

North
Fork Road

Gallatin River

Lone
Mountain
Ranch

to Highway 191

Paved Road	———
Dirt Road	= = = =
Main Ski Trail	▬▬▬
Additional Ski Trails	• • • •
River/Creek	———

North Fork Trail Elevation Profile

9000'
8500'
8000'
7500'
7000'
0 mi   1.0 mi   2.0 mi   3.0 mi   4.0 mi   5.0 mi   6.0 mi   7.0 mi   8.0 mi   9.0 mi   10.0 mi

GALLATIN CANYON

7 : North Fork/Bear Basin Trail

Distance: 3.8 to 10 miles round trip

Elevation Gain: 300 to 1,667 feet

Topo Maps: USGS: Gallatin Peak
Beartooth Publishing: "Bozeman, Big Sky to West"

Trail Report: There are a lot of options, in terms of length on this trail. The lower part travels through open conifers, within site of North Fork Creek. The trail then climbs into the spectacular Bear Basin where it is surrounded by towering granite cliff walls.

Getting There: From Bozeman take Huffine Lane west 6 miles to Four Corners. Turn left (south) on Highway 191 and continue 33.8 miles to the Big Sky turnoff. Turn right (west) and follow the road 4.8 miles. Turn right on North Fork Road and continue .8 miles to the signed trailhead.

Skiing: The first 0.75 miles is downhill on an old road, then after crossing a gravel road, begin a gentle, steady climb to the bridge at 1.9 miles. The bridge over North Fork Creek is a great place to turn around, but those wanting a longer ski can continue up the trail on the other side of the creek.

The trees get more dense as the trail continues its gradual climb to the junction with trail 402 at 3 miles. (Trail 402 eventually leads to the Beehive Basin Trail). This is another good turn around spot.

After this junction the trail begins to get a bit steeper. At 5 miles, you'll pop out into stunning Bear Basin, a place worth the climb. The basin is about a mile long and warrants a little touring—no need to stay on the trail—before heading back to the trailhead.

Taking it Further: If you are on backcountry skis, the possibilities are wide open for touring around Bear Basin.

Snowshoeing: This trail is nice for snowshoeing, but there isn't a lot of opportunity to leave the trail until reaching the basin.

Noteworthy Views: Bear Basin isn't as popular as nearby Beehive Basin—perhaps because it is a longer approach—but it rivals Beehive in spectacular views.

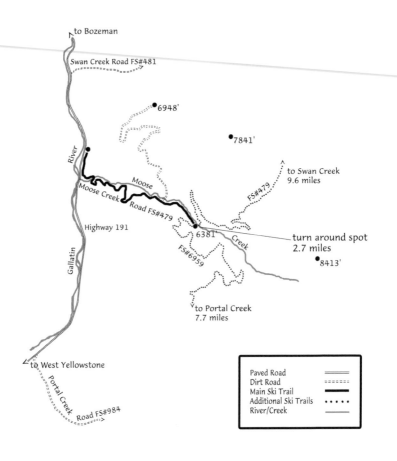

to Bozeman

Swan Creek Road FS#481

•6948'

•7841'

River

to Swan Creek
9.6 miles

FS#479

Moose

Moose Creek

Road FS#479

Highway 191

Gallatin

6381'

Creek

turn around spot
2.7 miles

•8413'

FS#6959

to Portal Creek
7.7 miles

to West Yellowstone

Portal Creek

Road FS#984

Paved Road	———
Dirt Road	=======
Main Ski Trail	▬▬▬
Additional Ski Trails	• • • • •
River/Creek	———

Moose Creek Road Elevation Profile

7200'
6800'
6400'
6000'
5600'

0 mi   0.5 mi   1.0 mi   1.5 mi   2.0 mi   2.5 mi   3.0 mi   3.5 mi   4.0 mi   4.5 mi   5.0 mi   5.5 mi

8 : Moose Creek Road

Distance: 5.4 miles round trip

Elevation Gain: 665 feet

Topo Maps: USGS: Hidden Lake
Beartooth Publishing: "Bozeman, Big Sky to West"

Trail Report: Not a spectacular trail, this ski makes for a good, quick workout. It is easy to access and it is a good place for a short ski on the way through the Gallatin Canyon.

Getting There: From Bozeman take Huffine Lane west 6 miles to Four Corners. Turn left (south) on Highway 191 and continue 25 miles to a large pullout on the left (east) at the signed Moose Creek Road.

Skiing: Begin skiing up the road, steadily climbing through spruce and pine forest. Moose Creek Road parallels the highway and the Gallatin River for the first 0.4 miles. The road then turns east, crosses Moose Creek and climbs up the south side of the creek.

The road continues uphill through forests and meadows. Snowmobilers and other skiers often cut the switchbacks making the ski a little steeper, but shorter. Eventually views across the valley into the Madison Range are gained. After 2.7 miles the road dead-ends at Forest Service Road 6959. This is our turn around spot. Enjoy the easy, but quick ski back down to the vehicle.

With Kids: This is a good trail to take the kids on. The road is enough of a climb to gain a sense of accomplishment, but not too steep. Also, there is good snowball fighting (or snowman building) terrain towards the top. Snowmobiles use the road, too, so be alert around corners.

Taking it Further: To extend the trip continue either direction on Road 6959 from the turn around point. To the left, the road eventually connects with the Swan Creek Trail, and to the right it meets with Portal Creek Road.

Snowshoeing: Snowshoeing is definitely possible here, but kind of boring until you get up higher and can get off the road.

Nature Notes: Although called the Moose Creek Road, moose are not likely to be seen here since they generally hang out in willows near creeks and wetlands and this road stays above the creek. As you gain elevation, look down into Moose Creek or across the canyon for your best shot at spotting moose. It's been said that dried moose pellets give off a lovely pine scent when burned as incense.

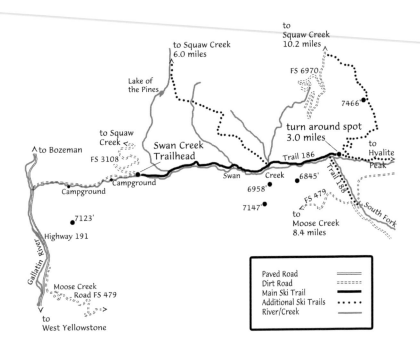

to
Squaw Creek
10.2 miles

to Squaw Creek
6.0 miles

FS 6970

7466'

Lake of
the Pines

turn around spot
3.0 miles

to Squaw
Creek

Swan Creek
Trailhead

to Hyalite
Peak

to Bozeman

FS 3108

Trail 186

Swan   Creek

6845'

Campground

Campground

6958'

7147'

7123'

to
Moose Creek
8.4 miles

South Fork

FS 479

Trail 188

Highway 191

Gallatin River

Moose Creek
Road FS 479

to
West Yellowstone

Paved Road	———
Dirt Road	=======
Main Ski Trail	▬▬▬
Additional Ski Trails	••••••
River/Creek	———

GALLATIN CANYON

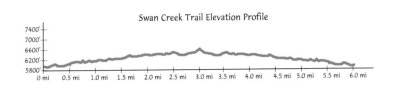

Swan Creek Trail Elevation Profile

7400'
7000'
6600'
6200'
5800'

0 mi   0.5 mi   1.0 mi   1.5 mi   2.0 mi   2.5 mi   3.0 mi   3.5 mi   4.0 mi   4.5 mi   5.0 mi   5.5 mi   6.0 mi

9 : Swan Creek Trail

Distance: 6 miles round trip

Elevation Gain: 520 feet

Topo Maps: USGS: Hidden Lake, Garnet Mountain, Mt.
Blackmore & The Sentinel
Beartooth Publishing: "Bozeman, Big Sky to West"

Trail Report: This undulating ski follows Swan Creek through meadows, past beaver lodges and in and out of conifers. With no real end destination, the trail length can be adapted to whatever you feel like doing.

Getting There: From Bozeman take Huffine Lane west 6 miles to Four Corners. Turn left (south) on Highway 191 and continue 25 miles to the Swan Creek turnoff on the left. You'll probably have to park just off the highway as the road to the trailhead is often snowed in. If possible, drive to road's end (1.5 miles).

Skiing: Either ski up the road 1.5 miles, or from the trailhead, ski east on the wide path through the willows. The trail soon narrows. At 0.4 miles the trail jogs up a steep hill (an interesting descent in icy conditions).

At 1.5 miles, a trail veers off to the left, which hooks up with logging roads and winds up in Squaw Creek. Make a right and then a quick left at the "trail" sign.

At 3 miles there is another trail junction. This is our turn around point. From here, ski back the way you came, or try a foray up one of the many logging roads in the area.

With Kids: Even though this trail does not gain a lot of elevation overall, there are a lot of ups and downs, often on very narrow single track. There are better places for kids to ski.

Snowshoeing: There are lots of options for snowshoeing, both on the described trail and off the trail. Choose a path and follow it.

Taking it Further: At the 3-mile junction, the right trail follows the South Fork Swan Creek a short way before ending at a logging road that heads over to Moose Creek. Just beyond the three mile trail junction lays another. Stay right. The left trail hooks into the same logging roads as the trail at the first junction. The right-hand trail continues to follow the creek until the 7-mile mark where it starts to steeply climb towards Hyalite Peak. This is the other turn around option.

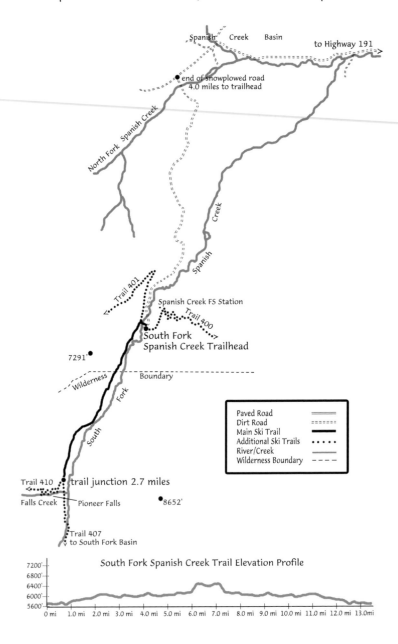

Spanish Creek Basin

to Highway 191

end of snowplowed road
4.0 miles to trailhead

North Fork Spanish Creek

Spanish Creek

Trail 401

Spanish Creek FS Station

Trail 400

South Fork
Spanish Creek Trailhead

7291'

Wilderness   Boundary

South Fork

Paved Road	══════
Dirt Road	======
Main Ski Trail	▬▬▬▬
Additional Ski Trails	• • • •
River/Creek	▬▬▬▬
Wilderness Boundary	— — —

Trail 410

trail junction 2.7 miles

Falls Creek   Pioneer Falls   8652'

Trail 407
to South Fork Basin

South Fork Spanish Creek Trail Elevation Profile

7200'
6800'
6400'
6000'
5600'

0 mi   1.0 mi   2.0 mi   3.0 mi   4.0 mi   5.0 mi   6.0 mi   7.0 mi   8.0 mi   9.0 mi   10.0 mi   11.0 mi   12.0 mi   13.0mi

GALLATIN CANYON

10 : South Fork Spanish Creek Trail

Distance: 5.4 to 13.4 miles round trip
(depending on starting point)

Elevation Gain: 300 feet from trailhead:
735 feet from parking area on road

Topo Maps: USGS: Beacon Point & Willow Swamp
Beartooth Publishing: "Bozeman, Big Sky to West"

Trail Report: Depending on the amount of snow on the ground, there are two possibilities for this tour. If it snows as much as ski bunnies hope, driving to the trailhead may be impossible. In this case park at the gate at the end of Ted Turner's Flying D Ranch road and the beginning of the Forest Service road. Then ski up the road.

Getting There: From Bozeman take Huffine Lane west 6 miles to Four Corners. Turn left (south) on Highway 191 and continue 13.1 miles to Spanish Creek Rd. on the right. Turn right. From Big Sky, Spanish Creek Road is 20.7 miles north on Highway 191, on the left.

Drive 5.3 miles to the end of the plowed road. Here Ted Turner's Flying D Ranch road ends and the Forest Service road begins. Either ski or drive, depending on conditions, the gradually ascending road through Turner's 113,600-acre ranch looking for bison, coyotes and wolves along the way. After 4 miles you'll reach the trailhead and can either continue up the trail or turn around and glide back to your vehicle.

Photo © Kyle Mace.
Looking up Spanish Creek.

Skiing: From the west end of the trailhead parking lot, cross the bridge over the South Fork of Spanish Creek and turn left. The very gradual trail follows the creek 2.7 miles to a marked junction. This is our turn around point.

With Kids: Spanish Creek is an ideal place to ski with kids. The ski up the road is almost as lovely as the trail route. Lucky skiers may see bison in the sagebrush off the road. The ski along the trail is mellow and open.

Taking it Further: At the junction turn right (west) and continue .75 miles up switchbacks to 40-foot Pioneer Falls, but only if you are well versed in avalanche conditions, as the trail gets substantially steeper. The ski can be quick on the way out and if the snow coverage isn't great, plan to hop over rocky sections of the trail.

Alternatively, continue straight (south) on the trail from the junction and continue into the South Fork basin. This is the route backcountry skiers use to access Blaze Mountain (10,384 feet) in late spring and early summer.

Snowshoeing: The trail is an easy snowshoe and there are plenty of opportunities to head off the trails into the woods. Snowshoes are a better way to access Pioneer Falls if you don't mind walking 3 miles to get to the trail.

Nature Notes: Moose often hang out in the willows along creeks, gnawing on last year's plants. Friends and I have been charged by a young moose here, so exercise caution when near the creek.

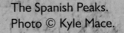

The Spanish Peaks.
Photo © Kyle Mace.

GALLATIN CANYON

Flying D Ranch

To get to the Spanish Creek trailhead, you'll have to drive through the Flying D Ranch owned by cable television billionaire Ted Turner. Now in his late 60s, Turner is the largest private landowner in America, and the 100,000 + acre Flying D is but one of his Montana ranches.

As with all his ranches, Turner has three goals for the Flying D: make money, protect the environment and promote conservation. The Flying D offers wealthy hunters the opportunity for trophy elk, sells bison meat (primarily through Ted's "Montana Grills"—there aren't actually any in Montana) and guides backcountry fishing.

Turner gave all the development rights of the Flying D to the Nature Conservancy, so it will stay undeveloped in perpetuity. Additionally, restoring native bison to the area aids in the restoration of native plants and animals.

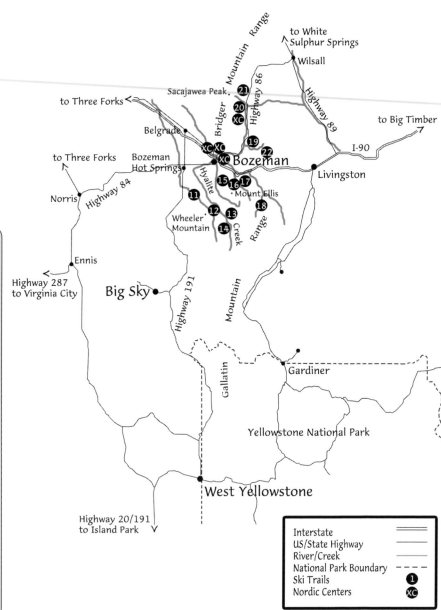

BOZEMAN AREA

BOZEMAN AREA

Bozeman is a thoroughly modern town that dates back to the 1880s. At its center are Montana State University and a thriving downtown. The lucky residents of Bozeman are surrounded by winter recreational opportunities.

From Bozeman one can see the ranges the tours in this book explore. To the north are the Bridger Mountains—Bozeman's local playground, named after famed mountain man Jim Bridger. To the south, the Gallatin Range climbs from agricultural fields to reach heights of over 10,000 feet.

John Bozeman abandoned his wife and children to move to Montana and try his luck at gold mining. The mine failed and he decided instead to "mine the miners". Bozeman is responsible for helping forge the Bozeman Trail (a cut-off on the Oregon Trail, it became known as the "Bloody Bozeman" due to all the murders that took place along its route) and laying out the town of Bozeman.

Many of the trails near the town of Bozeman enjoy popular use, but others are surprisingly vacant. Both busy and quiet trails offer scenic rewards, the opportunity to watch wildlife and a chance to stretch out one's muscles.

Looking northwest over Bozeman & the Gallatin Valley. Photo ©Tristin Dunlap.

BOZEMAN AREA

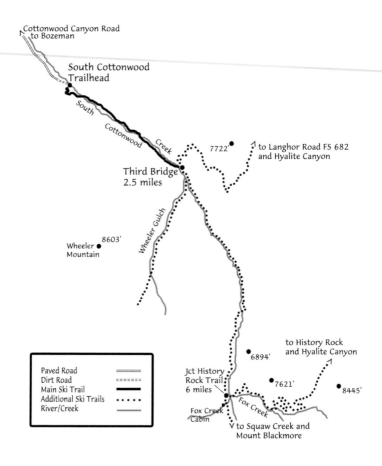

Cottonwood Canyon Road
to Bozeman

South Cottonwood
Trailhead

South
Cottonwood Creek

7722

to Langhor Road FS 682
and Hyalite Canyon

Third Bridge
2.5 miles

Wheeler Gulch

8603'

Wheeler
Mountain

to History Rock
and Hyalite Canyon

6894'

Jct History
Rock Trail
6 miles

7621'

8445'

Fox Creek
Cabin

Fox Creek

to Squaw Creek and
Mount Blackmore

Paved Road	
Dirt Road	=======
Main Ski Trail	
Additional Ski Trails	•••••••
River/Creek	

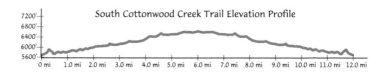

South Cottonwood Creek Trail Elevation Profile

7200'
6800'
6400'
6000'
5600'

0 mi   1.0 mi   2.0 mi   3.0 mi   4.0 mi   5.0 mi   6.0 mi   7.0 mi   8.0 mi   9.0 mi   10.0 mi   11.0 mi   12.0 mi

11 : South Cottonwood Creek

Distance: 5 miles round trip to third bridge;
12 miles round trip to History Rock Trail

Elevation Gain: 200 feet at 3rd bridge;
460 feet at History Rock Trail

Topo Maps: USGS: Wheeler Mountain
Beartooth Publishing: "Bozeman, Big Sky to West"

Trail Report: South Cottonwood Creek Trail is close to Bozeman and can get crowded on the weekends. This trail is best skied within a few days after it snows. But, if you don't mind sharing the trail and appreciate a well-packed path, this is the trail for you.

Getting There: From Bozeman drive 4 miles west on Huffine Lane to Cottonwood Creek Rd. Turn left and drive 7.6 miles to Cottonwood Canyon Road and turn left. Follow this road 2.1 miles until the road ends at the trailhead. Cottonwood Creek Road can also be reached by following South 19th Avenue past Hyalite Canyon.

Skiing: From the parking lot, look for the trailhead sign and follow the switchbacks 150 feet up the hill. After the climb, the trail descends through the trees to Cottonwood Creek. Cross the creek on the log bridge (extra credit for crossing with skis on) and herringbone or side-step up the steep, but short hill to continue on the mellow trail through meadows and forest.

The trail hugs an exposed hillside with South Cottonwood Creek below. This is a good place to spot moose from a safe distance. The trail crosses the creek again at 1.5 miles and a third time at 2.5 miles. Turn around here, or continue on to the junction of the History Rock Trail at 6 miles.

For those continuing along the trail from the third bridge, be prepared for steep switchbacks and a quick descent to the fourth bridge. The trail then crosses gentle meadows to the trail junction and a fifth bridge.

With Kids: This trail makes a great snowshoe or walk with kids, but it might be best to leave the skis at home.

Taking it Further: From the junction with the History Rock Trail it is 6 miles to the History Rock Trailhead, but it is a pretty steep climb to the Hyalite Divide, followed by a steep descent. The Fox Creek Forest Service cabin is located near the trail junction.

This trail also accesses Wheeler Mountain, a backcountry ski favorite. While you wouldn't want to tackle it on cross country skis, you can ski the start of the spur trail after crossing the third bridge. The trail heads off to the right (west) and is easily found if others have cut tracks that way.

Snowshoeing: From the trailhead follow the trail to the first bridge. Before crossing the bridge, head up the right (west) side of the creek. Make your own trail until linking back up with the main trail at the second bridge.

Building a "Quinzee" Snow Shelter

Spending time in the snow is a great way for families to bond, have fun and get some exercise. If you are planning to camp, or stay in a forest service cabin, building a snow shelter can keep the kids busy, provide an "extra room" and teach a valuable survival skill. Plus, a snow hut, or "quinzee" is fun to make.

First, clear a circular area in the snow about 7 or 8 feet across. Then, use a shovel or other digging tool to mix up the snow in the clearing, making sure to bring snow from bottom layers up higher and vice versa. Mixing snow of different temperatures will facilitate the hardening process.

Next, make a large pile (about 6 feet high) of snow on top of the clearing and shape it into a dome. The snow should be heaped, not packed. Allow the mound to sit for 3 to 5 hours.

When the snow is settled and hardened, hollow out the mound. Depending on the height of your pile, it is sometimes easier to start by digging a small stepped pit next to the mound where you want the door to be. Then, tunnel straight in at first to create your initial opening, then dig at an upward angle in order to make an elevated sleeping area inside the mound. This will allow cold air from inside to flow down and out of the shelter.

Use the snow you dig out to make a windbreak in front of the entrance, or heap it onto the exterior of the shelter to thicken its walls and increase the available interior space.

Smooth out the interior walls and ceiling when the hollowed area is large enough and poke a ventilation hole through the top of the dome using a ski pole or long stick. Make sure this hole stays clear of ice and snow.

Carve a bench along the wall to sleep on, then climb in and enjoy. It will be quite comfortable and quiet even in the coldest and most stormy weather.

BOZEMAN AREA

Hyalite Canyon.

Hyalite Canyon

The Hyalite drainage is a 34,000-acre watershed located between Gallatin Canyon and the Paradise Valley. It is surrounded by 10,000 foot peaks, creeks, streams, lakes and numerous waterfalls.

This popular recreation area is one of the premier ice climbing venues in the United States and is also popular with snowmobilers, backcountry skiers, ice fishermen (and women), as well as cross-country skiers and snowshoers. **www.hyalite.org**

Beginning in 2007, the Gallatin National Forest is in the process of implementing new travel plans for the entire forest. The Forest Service is working with Gallatin County, the City of Bozeman and user groups to secure funding to plow the Hyalite Road to the Blackmore Parking Lot at the reservoir until March 31st every season. This is great benefit as it turns what was once sketchy combat driving, known as the "Hyalite Rodeo," into a moderate winter drive accessing a veritable winter playground.

Hyalite Canyon is a beautiful place to be any time of the year. This book explores just a few of the many ski and snowshoe tours abounding in this area.

Getting There: From Main Street in Bozeman turn south on South 19th and drive 7 miles to Hyalite Canyon Road and a brown National Forest sign. Turn left and drive up the canyon, following the directions for individual tours.

Moose (Alces alces)

Of all winter wildlife, moose may be the most dangerous. They are big animals and aren't afraid to charge a skier (or skier's dog) if they feel threatened. It's especially important not to disturb wildlife in the winter as they have limited fat stores—and even more limited foraging opportunities—with which to survive this difficult season.

Moose generally hang out in forested habitats where lakes, marshes, and other wetlands provide them with aquatic vegetation and willows. But in less wet areas they also eat the woody browse in early stages of regrowth following disturbances like fires, logging, and clearing.

Often moose will travel on packed ski or snowmobile trails to reserve energy. If you see one, be quiet, control your dog and give them lots of space. In a narrow canyon this may mean cutting your tour short and turning around.

If a moose walks toward you it is not trying to be your friend, but rather to warn you off. If a moose does charge you, it may be a good idea to run or ski away, dodging in and out of trees (do not do this with bears, mountain lions or other predators). The moose will probably only chase you a short way. If it is stomping you, curl up in a tight ball, protect your head and don't get up until it goes away. Remember, moose don't want to eat you—they're herbivores—they just want to be left alone.

12 : Langohr Loop Trail

Distance: 0.03 to 2 miles round trip

Elevation Gain: negligible

Topo Maps: USGS: Wheeler Mountain
Beartooth Publishing: "Bozeman, Big Sky to West"

Trail Report: This super short ski is scenic and accessible to almost anyone. The trail winds through conifers and along Hyalite Creek. The loop is paved and provides wheelchair access in the summer.

Getting There: Travel 5.9 miles up Hyalite Creek Road to Langohr Campground on the right. Park along the road or any plowed pullouts.

Skiing: Ski into the campground, making an immediate right and heading 0.01 miles to the signed trailhead.

Cross the bridge over Hyalite Creek and turn left heading upstream. The trail ends quickly at a large rock formation. Return to the bridge and head downstream, closely following Hyalite Creek. At the fork—not far from the bridge—stay right. This is the beginning of the loop.

At the far end of the loop, the trail continues north, but this may or may not be obvious in the winter. The main trail loops around through forests and meadows until it reaches the top end of the loop. Continue straight, back to the bridge.

With Kids: Small children will love this ski. It is short, flat and winds through enchanted forest. The hillside on the east side of the road is a popular sledding and tubing spot.

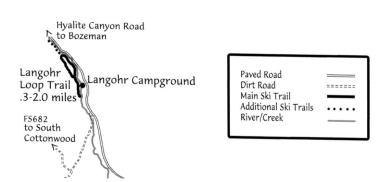

Paved Road	═══════
Dirt Road	=======
Main Ski Trail	▬▬▬▬
Additional Ski Trails	• • • •
River/Creek	─────

Hyalite Canyon Road
to Bozeman

Langohr
Loop Trail   Langohr Campground
.3-2.0 miles

FS682
to South
Cottonwood

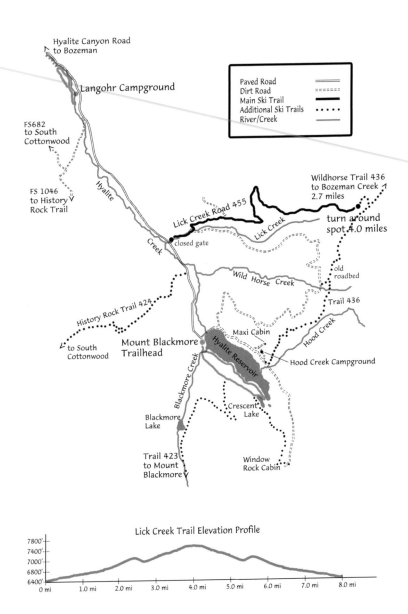

BOZEMAN AREA

Hyalite Canyon Road
to Bozeman

Langohr Campground

FS682
to South
Cottonwood

FS 1046
to History
Rock Trail

Hyalite Creek

Lick Creek Road 455
closed gate

Lick Creek

Wildhorse Trail 436
to Bozeman Creek
2.7 miles

turn around
spot 4.0 miles

old
roadbed

Wild Horse Creek

Trail 436

History Rock Trail 424

Maxi Cabin

Hood Creek

to South
Cottonwood

Mount Blackmore
Trailhead

Hyalite Reservoir

Hood Creek Campground

Blackmore Creek

Crescent
Lake

Blackmore
Lake

Trail 423
to Mount
Blackmore

Window
Rock Cabin

Legend

Paved Road	═══════
Dirt Road	=======
Main Ski Trail	▬▬▬▬▬
Additional Ski Trails	• • • • •
River/Creek	———

Lick Creek Trail Elevation Profile

7800'
7400'
7000'
6800'
6400'

0 mi   1.0 mi   2.0 mi   3.0 mi   4.0 mi   5.0 mi   6.0 mi   7.0 mi   8.0 mi

13 : Lick Creek Road

Distance: 8 miles round trip

Elevation Gain: 1,100 feet

Topo Maps: USGS: Wheeler Mountain & Mt. Ellis
Beartooth Publishing: "Bozeman, Big Sky to West"

Trail Report: This tour follows a closed road through treed and open areas with at least one great view of the Hyalite Peaks. Better known as a mountain biking trail, Lick Creek Road can provide a fun trip for skiers in Hyalite Canyon.

Getting There: Travel 8.2 miles up Hyalite Creek Road. Gated Lick Creek Road is on the left; there is room for two or three cars to park here in the winter.

Skiing: Ski around the gate and up the road. The road soon crosses Lick Creek twice as it steadily climbs for four miles. Ignore any spur roads or tracks leaving from the main road. The road becomes narrower towards the end—more of an ATV trail than a road. At four miles there is a sign for Lick Creek Road and a trail junction. This is our turn around point. Return the way you came, enjoying the quick descent.

With Kids: Since most of the tour is on an old road, it is a fairly mellow ski—not too steep, but a steady climb. The trip out can be quick in the right snow conditions, but should be manageable for most kid skiers.

Taking it Further: Lick Creek Road provides access to several other trails in the Hyalite and Bozeman Creek Drainages. From the junction and turn around point for this tour, the Wildhorse Trail (to the left) heads down to South Bozeman Creek and eventually to Mystic Lake. This route may be quite difficult to find in the winter.

Turning right at the junction onto Wildhorse Trail, one can follow a trail back into Hyalite Canyon. This route might also be challenging to locate in the snow.

The Bridger Ski Foundation (BSF) is working to expand their system of groomed trails and loops throughout Hyalite and linking up with other drainages. Look for updates at www.hyalite.org.

Snowshoeing: The road itself makes a nice exercise-walk, but might be a little boring for some snowshoers. Fortunately, there is always somewhere interesting to explore for the snowshoer. Walk up the road a bit until you see something interesting and head towards it.

Noteworthy Views: Great views of the Hyalite Peaks.

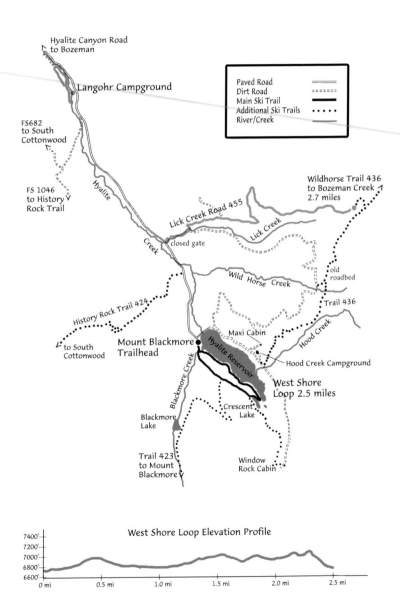

Hyalite Canyon Road
to Bozeman

Langohr Campground

Paved Road
Dirt Road
Main Ski Trail
Additional Ski Trails
River/Creek

FS682
to South
Cottonwood

FS 1046
to History
Rock Trail

Hyalite

Creek

Lick Creek Road 455

Lick Creek

Wildhorse Trail 436
to Bozeman Creek
2.7 miles

closed gate

Wild Horse Creek

old
roadbed

History Rock Trail 424

Trail 436

to South
Cottonwood

Maxi Cabin

Hood Creek

Mount Blackmore
Trailhead

Hyalite Reservoir

Hood Creek Campground

Blackmore Creek

West Shore
Loop 2.5 miles

Crescent
Lake

Blackmore
Lake

Trail 423
to Mount
Blackmore

Window
Rock Cabin

BOZEMAN AREA

West Shore Loop Elevation Profile

7400'
7200'
7000'
6800'
6600'

0 mi   0.5 mi   1.0 mi   1.5 mi   2.0 mi   2.5 mi

14 : West Shore Loop Trail

Distance: 2.5 mile loop

Elevation Gain: 240 feet

Topo Maps: USGS: Fridley Peak
Beartooth Publishing: "Bozeman, Big Sky to West"

Trail Report: A rolling trail along the shores of Hyalite Reservoir, this loop passes through forests, meadows and beside a small pond—Crescent Lake. This straightforward trail can somehow become a little confusing in the forest, especially if there aren't any tracks to follow.

Getting There: Travel 9.9 miles up Hyalite Creek Road to the reservoir and a parking area on the right side of the road.

Skiing: Start skiing on the Blackmore Trail on the north side of the parking lot—just to the right of a pit toilet. The trail is initially steep and narrow, but soon forms a junction with Crescent Trail.

At times there may be a groomed trail leading directly out of the south end of the Blackmore parking lot that leads directly to the Cresent Trail.

Ski southeast on the Cresent Trail following the trail through thick conifers to Crescent Lake, about half the distance of the tour.

The trail skirts around the southwest end of the lake, then curves to the left, towards Hyalite Reservoir. The trail curves again to the left and you are now skiing back the way you came, this time near the reservoir shore.

The trail undulates a lot in this section, eventually leading you to a bridge over Blackmore Creek. Cross the bridge and head into the trailhead parking lot.

With Kids: It's a fun jaunt through the forest that kids will likely enjoy. However the trail is narrow and has lots of small ups and downs.

Taking it Further: From the far end of the loop, just beyond Crescent Lake, a spur trail leads about 0.75 miles to the Window Rock Forest Service Cabin and Hyalite Canyon Road.

Snowshoeing: This is a great trail to snowshoe, maybe even more so than ski. It's pretty and serene and you often feel as if no one else is anywhere nearby.

History Hints: Hyalite reservoir was constructed in the late 1940s and enlarged in 1993. It is used for drinking water for the City of Bozeman and to irrigate the Gallatin Valley. The reservoir contains cutthroat trout and arctic grayling and is a popular ice fishing spot.

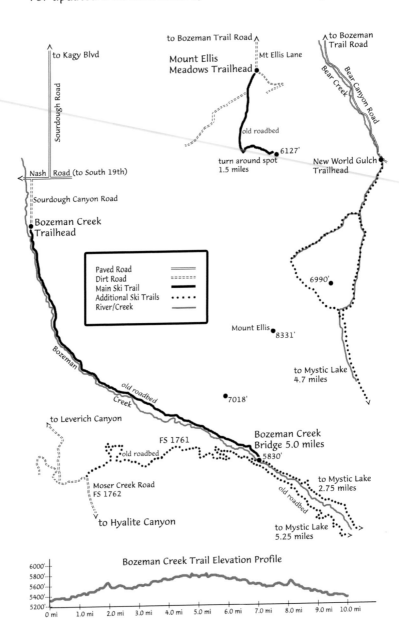

15 : Bozeman Creek Trail

Distance: 10 mile round trip

Elevation Gain: 500 feet

Topo Maps: USGS: Wheeler Mountain & Mount Ellis
Beartooth Publishing: "Bozeman, Big Sky to West"

Trail Report: Plan to see a lot of people and dogs on this trail as it is easily accessible from the town of Bozeman. The Bozeman Creek Trail, known locally as "Sourdough Trail" follows Bozeman Creek to Mystic Lake, where it links up with other trails. This tour covers the first half of the route, but eager skiers can easily continue on to the lake.

Up to 15kms of trail in Bozeman Creek are often groomed by the Bridger Ski Foundation. Check out their websites for more information or contacts: **www.bridgerskifoundation.com** or **www.bsfnordic.com**

Getting There: From Bozeman, drive south on Sourdough Road 3.8 miles from Kagy Boulevard to Nash Boulevard. Turn right on Nash and after 0.25 miles turn left at the Forest Service access sign onto Sourdough Canyon Road. Drive 0.9 miles to the trailhead. Nash is also accessible from South 19th Avenue before the Hyalite Road turn off.

Winter wonderland above the Bozeman Creek drainage.
Photo © Tristin Dunlap.

Skiing: From the south end of the parking area, ski around the gate and up the old logging road. This first mile or two of this tour can be packed out and icy, but continue on, knowing that better snow lies up the trail.

After passing the water monitoring station at about 0.75 miles, the trail heads uphill to the 1 mile marker. Above the creek now, the road meanders and alternates between gradual inclines and short hills until about 2.75 miles where it enters a flat spruce-fir parkland. There is an outhouse here, although it isn't usually stocked in the winter.

Continue skiing along the road until the trail drops down to a bridge over Bozeman Creek. This is the turn around point.

With Kids: There are almost always kids on this trail. The relatively easy terrain to the water monitoring station (0.75 miles) makes it a great ski for beginning skiers or those who prefer a shorter distance.

Taking it Further: After crossing the bridge, it is possible to continue on the road another 5.25 miles to Mystic Lake. A Forest Service cabin is available for rent. (For more on renting Forest Service cabins see page 15).

Avoid the trail to the left just before the bridge (unless you are snowshoeing). This trail is too gnarly for cross-country skiing.

Trails to New World Gulch (steep) and Bear Canyon leave from the lake. Additionally, the road you skied in on continues.

Snowshoeing: Tromping up the road may be a bit boring, but if you can make it to the bridge there is a single track trail that leads 2.75 miles to Mystic Lake. Locate the trail on the left of the main trail just before crossing the bridge.

Be aware of avalanche paths crossing the trail en route to Mystic Lake.

History Hints: Bozeman Creek is one of the three streams that supply more than half the water to Bozeman residents. Since the breaching of the Mystic Lake Dam in 1985, this is strictly a surface water source.

BOZEMAN AREA

16 : Mount Ellis Meadows

See Map on Page 66

Distance: 3 miles round trip

Elevation Gain: 840 feet

Topo Maps: USGS: Mount Ellis
Beartooth Publishing: "Bozeman, Big Sky to West"

Trail Report: Close to town, this is a popular escape for people wanting a quick ski, snowshoe or walk. On a nice weekend day, count on seeing a lot of people and a lot of dogs. This is one of the few trails in the book on State land rather than National Forest land.

Getting There: From Highway 90 in Bozeman, take the Bear Canyon exit and turn east onto Bozeman Trail. After 0.7 miles turn left on Mt. Ellis Lane. At 1.5 miles the road ends at a log arch. Park on either side of the road.

Skiing: Pass through the gate and ski straight up the wide, open hill about 1 mile. Here the trail enters the trees. Follow the trail to the left where it soon becomes an obvious logging road. The trail continues another 0.5 miles from the junction in the trees.

Return the way you came, preparing for a quick descent down the hill.

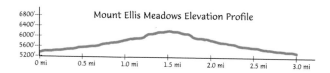

With Kids: This is a pretty good family ski as it is short and wide. The return ski is a little steep, but the hill is so open, that there is plenty of room to make big turns, and there is almost always unskied snow to slow you down.

Snowshoeing: Lots of people snowshoe here. The first mile is a bit of a trudge, but once in the trees it is nice. It is possible to go right at the junction and explore that direction.

Noteworthy Views: Most of Bozeman, the Bridger Mountains, the Bangtail Range, the Tobacco Root Mountains, and parts of the Gallatin Mountains are viewed from here.

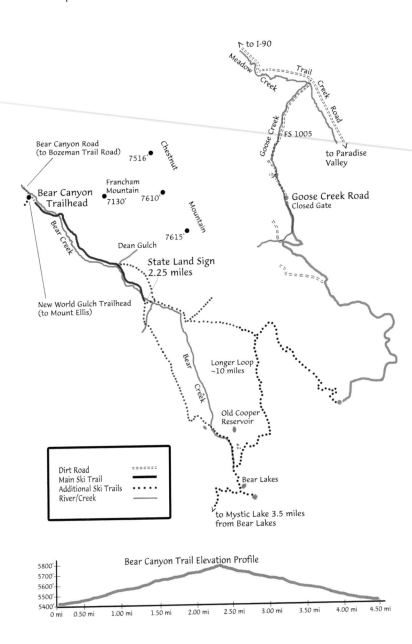

BOZEMAN AREA

to I-90

Meadow Creek Trail
Creek Road
to Paradise Valley

Goose Creek
FS 1005

Goose Creek Road
Closed Gate

Bear Canyon Road
(to Bozeman Trail Road)
7516'
Chestnut

Franchani
Mountain
7130'
7610'

Bear Canyon
Trailhead

Mountain

Bear Creek

Dean Gulch
7615'

State Land Sign
2.25 miles

New World Gulch Trailhead
(to Mount Ellis)

Bear Creek

Longer Loop
~10 miles

Old Cooper
Reservoir

Dirt Road
Main Ski Trail
Additional Ski Trails
River/Creek

Bear Lakes

to Mystic Lake 3.5 miles
from Bear Lakes

Bear Canyon Trail Elevation Profile
5800'
5700'
5600'
5500'
5400'
0 mi   0.50 mi   1.00 mi   1.50 mi   2.00 mi   2.50 mi   3.00 mi   3.50 mi   4.00 mi   4.50 mi

17 : Bear Canyon Trail

Distance: 4.5 miles round trip

Elevation Gain: 400 feet

Topo Maps: USGS: Mount Ellis & Bald Knob
Beartooth Publishing: "Bozeman, Big Sky to West"

Trail Report: When the snow is good, this is a great trail with opportunities for a short ski or an all-day adventure in beautiful, wintry surroundings. When it hasn't snowed for a while and the weather is warm, the lower section of trail can be icy and treacherous since there are often many people skiing both directions on a narrow trail.

The tour described below is a short out and back—with lots of options for taking it further—that ventures through wooded areas, meadows and a lovely riparian environment.

Getting There: From Bozeman, hop on Interstate 90 heading east. Exit at Bear Canyon Road and turn right. After 0.2 miles, turn left on Bear Canyon Road and drive 3.5 miles to the parking area on the right.

Skiing: From the parking area, ski or walk up the road in the same direction you were driving. After a couple minutes you will come to the trailhead next to the old ski area.

Looking south toward Bear Canyon, Ellis Meadow & Bozeman Creek.
Photo © Tristin Dunlap.

Ski along an old jeep road that narrows after a short distance. After about 0.75 miles the trail crosses the creek on a new bridge. Continue up the creek past three switchbacks to the State Land map and a trail heading south toward the Old Cooper Reservoir (read more about this in "Taking it Further"). This is our turn around point.

With Kids: This is a fun trail for kids when the snow is decent. On a warm, snowy day plan to see families, dogs and groups on the trail.

Taking it Further: From the State Lands sign and map, ski south up the trail, through thick trees and chirping chickadees. This trail eventually goes past Old Cooper Reservoir then heads north along an old road then back northwest to create a large loop (about 10 miles) ending at the bridge just east of the State Lands sign. Make sure you know where you are going because this trail gets used by snowmobilers (who tend to play around and not stick to the trail—causing various "user trails") and can be hard to follow.

Snowshoeing: Snowshoeing is OK on the Bear Creek Trail, and gets better, the further up you go. A better option, however, is to head up the New World Gulch Trail that is accessed from the parking lot. This is a popular trail for backcountry skiers to access Mt. Ellis.

Nature Notes: Two species of chickadees can be found in the area— Mountain and Black-Capped. Chickadees are one of the few songbirds that don't migrate in the winter. On the chilliest of winter nights, these birds can become radically hypothermic by dropping their body temperature 50 to 53.6° F below their normal daytime body temperature. Naturally, this means incredible energy savings. Being able to achieve this is one of the reasons chickadees do not have to migrate south. In fact, their year-round residency and hardiness has inspired some to argue that the Black Capped Chickadee should be the Montana State Bird.

History Hints: Much of this area, especially heading towards Goose Creek, is and was logged. Douglas-firs from the north end of the Gallatin Range can be found in many of the older houses in Bozeman and surrounding areas.

Bear Canyon Trail Changes

The old logging road on the west side of the creek has long been a slumping mess full of mud holes. Thus, in the summer of 2007, the Forest Service moved much of the lower trail to the east side of the creek where more stable limestone soils are found. Due to disputes between the Forest Service and Gallatin County, the old road may or may not remain open for travel. There will be even more trail improvements throughout Bear Canyon starting in 2008 so don't be surprised if signs or trails change.

BOZEMAN AREA

Getting off the beaten path near Bozeman.
Photo © Bob Allen Photography.

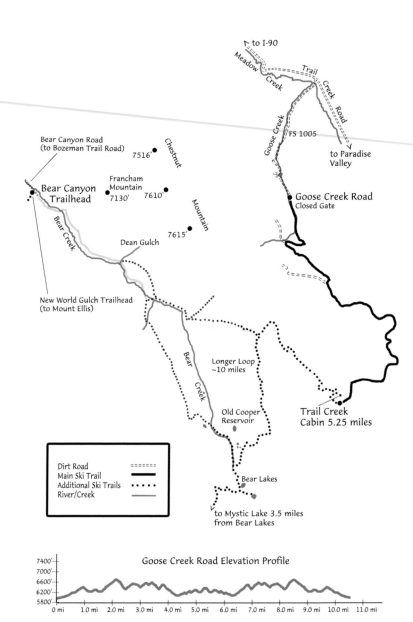

BOZEMAN AREA

to I-90

Meadow Creek Trail

Goose Creek

Trail Creek Road

FS 1005

to Paradise Valley

Bear Canyon Road
(to Bozeman Trail Road)

7516' Chestnut

Bear Canyon Trailhead

Goose Creek Road
Closed Gate

Francham Mountain
7130'   7610'

Mountain

7615'

Bear Creek

Dean Gulch

New World Gulch Trailhead
(to Mount Ellis)

Bear Creek

Longer Loop
~10 miles

Old Cooper Reservoir

Trail Creek
Cabin 5.25 miles

Dirt Road
Main Ski Trail
Additional Ski Trails
River/Creek

Bear Lakes

to Mystic Lake 3.5 miles
from Bear Lakes

Goose Creek Road Elevation Profile

7400'
7000'
6600'
6200'
5800'

0 mi 1.0 mi 2.0 mi 3.0 mi 4.0 mi 5.0 mi 6.0 mi 7.0 mi 8.0 mi 9.0 mi 10.0 mi 11.0 mi

18 : Goose Creek Road

Distance: 10.5 miles round trip

Elevation Gain: 300 feet

Topo Maps: USGS: Bald Knob
Beartooth Publishing: "Bozeman, Big Sky to West"

Trail Report: This tour follows a logging road through clear cuts and treed stretches to the Trail Creek Forest Service Cabin. (See page 15 for more information on renting cabins).

This tour follows the road 5.25 miles, but turn around anywhere the mood hits.

Getting There: Drive east on Interstate 90 from Bozeman, exiting at Trail Creek. Turn right off the exit ramp, cross the railroad tracks and follow the road left for 3 miles to Goose Creek Road.

Turn right and continue 2 miles to where the road is closed at a gate. The last section of road can be a little sketchy if there is a lot of snow, so park lower if necessary.

Skiing: Pass the gate and ski up the road. At 1 and 1.9 miles there are spur roads to the right. Ignore them and continue up the main road 5.25 miles to the cabin. (There is a shorter route to the cabin via Newman Creek, but for cross-country skiers, this route is easier, if longer.)

From the cabin, return the way you came, enjoying a fun glide back to your vehicle.

With Kids: A mellow ski that most anyone can handle, this tour is great for all abilities and ages. There may be snowmobiles on this route, especially on weekends, so stay alert.

Taking it Further: It is possible to make a cabin-to-cabin trip starting from the Trail Creek cabin at the end of this tour. The route to the Mystic Lake cabin starts on the logging road, but soon switches to a trail past the Old Cougar Reservoir and Bear Lakes (6-8 miles depending on the route). The section between Bear Lakes and the ridge is very steep and skiers will need skins. Because this area gets used by snowmobilers, there may be tracks all over the place—make sure you know where you are going.

From the Mystic Lake cabin it's a shorter (5.3 miles), but steep ski out New World Gulch Trail—with the possibility of sneaking in some turns on Mt. Ellis—or a mellow tour (10 miles) on the logging road following Bozeman Creek.

Snowshoeing: Go somewhere else, no sense trudging up a logging road.

BOZEMAN AREA

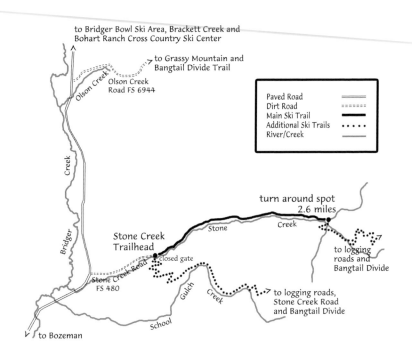

to Bridger Bowl Ski Area, Brackett Creek and
Bohart Ranch Cross Country Ski Center

to Grassy Mountain and
Bangtail Divide Trail

Olson Creek
Road FS 6944

Olson Creek

Creek

Bridger

turn around spot
2.6 miles

Stone Creek
Trailhead

Stone   Creek

closed gate

Stone Creek Road
FS 480

to logging
roads and
Bangtail Divide

Gulch

Creek

to logging roads,
Stone Creek Road
and Bangtail Divide

School

to Bozeman

Paved Road
Dirt Road
Main Ski Trail
Additional Ski Trails
River/Creek

Stone Creek Trail Elevation Profile

6400'
6200'
6000'
5800'
5600'

0 mi   0.5 mi   1.0 mi   1.5 mi   2.0 mi   2.5 mi   3.0 mi   3.5 mi   4.0 mi   4.5 mi   5.0 mi

19 : Stone Creek Road

Distance: 5.2 miles round trip

Elevation Gain: 540 feet

Topo Maps: USGS: Saddle Mountain & Grassy Mountain
Beartooth Publishing: "Bozeman, Big Sky to West"

Trail Report: This mellow tour follows a logging road and parallels Stone Creek as it heads up a drainage in the Bangtail Range.

Getting There: From Bozeman, drive north on North Rouse Avenue. The road becomes Bridger Canyon Road and winds through Bridger Canyon. Stone Creek Road is on the right, 12 miles from Main Street. Turn right and either park just over the cattle guards, or continue 1.2 miles to the trailhead parking at the Forest Service gate.

Skiing: Ski past the gate (or 1.2 miles up the road to the gate if you parked at the turn-off from Bridger Canyon Road) and along the vehicle restricted logging road. After two miles, the road turns sharply to the right. This is our turn around point, ski back the same way.

With Kids: This is a great tour for kids as it has little elevation gain and is easy to follow.

Taking it Further: From the turn around point, the road continues on and divides several times. It is possible to get in a full day of skiing by exploring the various forks in the road.

Snowshoeing: Snowshoers might explore the popular mountain bike trail that leaves from the same parking area as the ski tour. Look for the trail to the right, just before the gate.

Nature Notes: Known popularly as the Bangtail Range, these low mountains are probably better described as the east side of the Bridger Range.

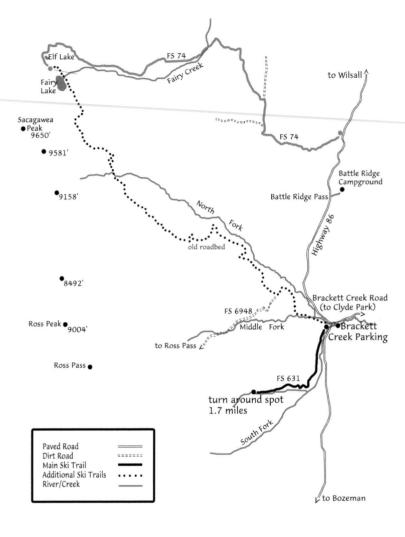

BOZEMAN AREA

Elf Lake

FS 74

Fairy Creek

to Wilsall

Fairy Lake

FS 74

Sacagawea
● Peak
9650'

Battle Ridge
Campground

● 9581'

Battle Ridge Pass

● 9158'

North

Fork

Highway 86

old roadbed

● 8492'

Brackett Creek Road
(to Clyde Park)

FS 6948

● Brackett
Creek Parking

Ross Peak ●
9004'

Middle   Fork

to Ross Pass

FS 631

turn around spot
1.7 miles

Ross Pass ●

South Fork

Paved Road
Dirt Road
Main Ski Trail
Additional Ski Trails
River/Creek

to Bozeman

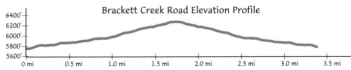

Brackett Creek Road Elevation Profile

6400'
6200'
6000'
5800'
5600'

0 mi   0.5 mi   1.0 mi   1.5 mi   2.0 mi   2.5 mi   3.0 mi   3.5 mi

78

20 : Brackett Creek Road

Distance: 3.4 miles round trip

Elevation Gain: 480 feet

Topo Maps: USGS: Saddle Peak
Beartooth Publishing: "Bozeman, Big Sky to West"

Trail Report: This is a popular cross-country ski trail for Bozeman residents. It's scenic, snowmobile-free and loaded with options.

Getting There: From Bozeman, drive north on North Rouse Avenue. The road becomes Bridger Canyon Road and winds through Bridger Canyon passing Bridger Bowl and Bohart Ranch Cross Country Ski Center. After 19 miles, turn right on Brackett Creek Road, cross a bridge and park in the parking lot on the right.

Looking north across the Bridger Range toward Brackett Creek.
Photo © Tristin Dunlap.

BOZEMAN AREA

Skiing: Exit the parking area, turn left on Brackett Creek Road and walk (or ski) back to Bridger Canyon Road. The tour starts on the other side of Bridger Canyon Road, directly across from its intersection with Brackett Creek Road.

Ski around the gate and head up the road. Starting out flat, the road quickly climbs a small hill and moves into the trees and away from Bridger Canyon Road.

Continue following the road as it consistently climbs to a small drainage at 1.7 miles. This is our turn around point, but read the "Taking it Further" section for more options.

With Kids: Bring the kids, bring the dogs, everyone shows up at the Brackett Creek Trail.

Taking it Further: The Brackett Creek area is best explored on one's own, as there are often many skier-made trails.

At the turn around point there are usually a couple skier-made trails. On the far side (southwest) of the drainage, head up the trail as it narrows through thick trees and then pops out into a meadow. Soon after, look for a trail to the right that heads back to the turn around point.

Instead of taking the trail to the right and thus returning to the turn around point, head straight ahead to a great view of the Bridgers or to the left to climb a small ridge.

Snowshoeing: There are lots of options for exploring on snowshoes in the Brackett Creek area. Start on the road as described above, then venture off to the right wherever it looks interesting.

Snowshoers may also enjoy the Grassy Mountain Trail that leaves from the south end of the parking area. This trail switchbacks up the hillside then traverses along a ridge.

History Hints: The Bridger range, along with other places, and countless local dogs and children, was named for the famous mountain man and trapper Jim Bridger. Bridger was best known for telling tall tales about glass mountains, "peetrified" birds singing "peetrified" songs, and the days when Pikes Peak was just a hole in the ground.

Noteworthy Views: For those willing to explore, there are great views of the Bridger Range and across to the Crazy Mountains.

Snowshoeing in Brackett Creek.
Photo © Bob Allen Photography.

For updated trail information, visit www.firstascentpress.com

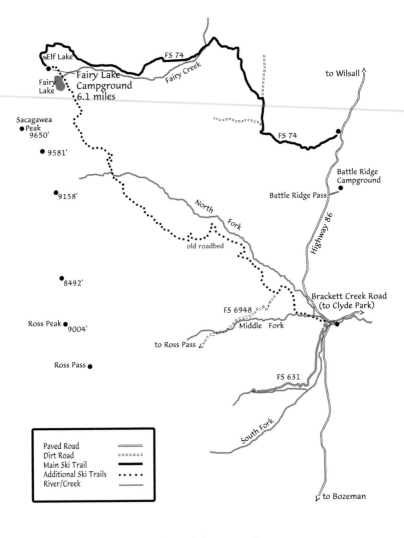

Elf Lake
FS 74
Fairy Creek
to Wilsall
Fairy Lake
Fairy Lake
Campground
6.1 miles
FS 74
Sacagawea
Peak
9650'
9581'
Battle Ridge
Campground
9158'
Battle Ridge Pass
North
Fork
Highway 86
old roadbed
8492'
Brackett Creek Road
(to Clyde Park)
FS 6948
Ross Peak
9004'
Middle Fork
to Ross Pass
Ross Pass
FS 631
South Fork

Paved Road
Dirt Road
Main Ski Trail
Additional Ski Trails
River/Creek

to Bozeman

BOZEMAN AREA

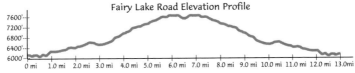

Fairy Lake Road Elevation Profile

82

21 : Fairy Lake Trail

Distance: 12.2 miles round trip

Elevation Gain: 1,400 feet

Topo Maps: USGS: Sacagawea Peak
  Beartooth Publishing: "Bozeman, Big Sky to West"

Trail Report: The Fairy Lake Road is often used by snowmobilers—many of whom are backcountry skiers looking for quick access to the east side of the Bridger Range. However, if a nice long ski on a road is what you are looking for—or if you are pulling a kid carrier and need to avoid single track trails—this may be the tour for you. Ski on weekdays to avoid many of the snowmobiles.

Getting There: From Bozeman, drive north on North Rouse Avenue. The road becomes Bridger Canyon Road and winds through Bridger Canyon passing Bridger Bowl and Bohart Ranch Cross Country Ski Center. After 21.5 miles (just past the Battle Ridge Campground) look for Fairy Lake Road on the left. Park just beyond the turn-off on the right.

Catching some telé turns.
Photo © Mariann Van Den Elzen.

Skiing: Ski past the gate and head up the road as it undulates and winds through meadows and treed areas. At 1.4 miles a spur road leads off to the left—ignore it. Just beyond the spur road, the main road cross the creek. At 1.8 miles bear left (a spur road goes right, but is often not visible in the winter).

The road crosses the creek again at 3.2 miles. At 5.7 miles you'll see the trail to Frazier Lake. Continue on the main road to the Fairy Lake Campground and the Fairy Lake and Sacagawea Peak trailheads. This is our turn around point. Ski back the way you came.

With Kids: Skiing on roads can be a great option for kids, and this tour is no exception. The route is easy to find and broad enough to allow for wide snowplows and some turning. There are a few sections that are fairly steep, considering this is a road, but they are short and fun to play around on. Meadows along the route also make great places to create snowmen or take a break from skiing. Of course, the whole tour might be a bit long for most kids.

Taking it Further: From our turn around point it is 0.25 mile to Fairy Lake and probably best accessed by walking. The lake is pretty and worth a look if you've already skied 6.1 miles to get to the trailhead.

Backcountry skiers access the cirque on the northwest side of Sacagawea Peak from the Sacagawea Peak Trailhead, but it is too steep and full of switchbacks for cross-country skiers.

Snowshoeing: There are lots of places to leave the road and snowshoe, but there are better places in the Bridgers to snowshoe, such as Brackett Creek, from the Battle Ridge Campground or any of the west side trails (see page 85).

Nature Notes: Mountain Goats may be seen on the Bridger Ridge. Because this tour stays low, binoculars may be helpful. Additionally, the Bridger Range hosts the largest known Golden Eagle migration in the United States. On average, 1,500 Golden Eagles migrate through here each fall.

BOZEMAN AREA

Snowshoeing in the Bridgers

In addition to the ski trails in the Bridger Mountains, there are many trails that are ideal for snowshoeing. In fact, there are probably more trails suited to snowshoeing than cross-country skiing; especially on the west side.

Grab a map to locate these excellent and scenic west side trails, just minutes from downtown Bozeman. Note that many of these trails enter avalanche terrain the higher you go.

Sypes Canyon Trail—4 miles round trip

This trailhead is located amongst an ever growing throng of houses, but feels fairly wild once you get up the trail a bit. The trail, squeezed between two fences, starts out flat and then quickly climbs the side of hill.

The trail climbs up the canyon and heads into a lodgepole forest after about 1 mile. Then it pops up onto a saddle overlooking the Gallatin Valley. Turn around here or; walk up the hill to the right about 200 yards for another vista, or; head left onto the Foothills Trail, which connects with the "M" Trail to the south and Middle Cottonwood to the north.

Middle Cottonwood Trail—mileage varies

The road to Middle Cottonwood might be a bit sketchy if there is a lot of snow, so park as soon as you need to and snowshoe up the road to the trailhead. The trail follows Cottonwood Creek up the canyon, mostly staying in the trees. At 1 mile you'll see the junction with the Foothills Trail (6 miles to the "M" Trail).

After the junction, the trail switchbacks up the mountain to a ridge at 1.4 miles. From here, enjoy the view up and down the canyon. The trail continues up the face of the hill to a cirque, and eventually a divide below Saddle Peak (about 5 miles). You can also access Truman Gulch by continuing this direction.

Truman Gulch Trail—4 miles round trip

The road to Truman Gulch used to be a real rollercoaster of a ride, not really suited for low clearance vehicles. It has gotten better, but you'll probably have to park a bit before the trailhead in the winter. The Truman Gluch Trail follows the creek, crossing it several times before reaching a clearing at 2 miles. From here the trail continues up the canyon and meets with the Foothills Trail where you can head south to Cottonwood Creek Trail or north into the Bridgers.

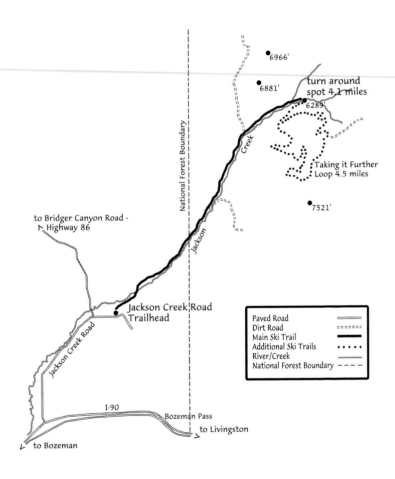

6966'

6881'

turn around
spot 4.1 miles

6289'

National Forest Boundary

Jackson Creek

Taking it Further
Loop 4.5 miles

7521'

to Bridger Canyon Road -
Highway 86

Jackson Creek Road
Trailhead

Jackson Creek Road

Paved Road	
Dirt Road	=======
Main Ski Trail	▬▬▬▬
Additional Ski Trails	•••••
River/Creek	
National Forest Boundary	– – –

I-90

Bozeman Pass

to Livingston

to Bozeman

BOZEMAN AREA

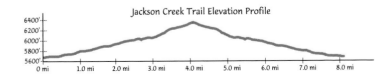

Jackson Creek Trail Elevation Profile

6400'
6200'
6000'
5800'
5600'

0 mi   1.0 mi   2.0 mi   3.0 mi   4.0 mi   5.0 mi   6.0 mi   7.0 mi   8.0 mi

22 : Jackson Creek Road

Distance: 8.2 miles round trip

Elevation Gain: 690 feet

Topo Maps: USGS: Bozeman Pass
Beartooth Publishing: "Bozeman, Big Sky to West"

Trail Report: The Jackson Creek Trail is actually old logging roads winding through hayfields (at first) and into open sage and conifers, following Jackson Creek. The farther you ski, the thicker the trees get. There are snowmobiles out here at times, but weekdays are a safe bet if you want to avoid them.

Getting There: From Livingston drive west on Interstate 90 for 12 miles (from Bozeman, 10 miles east) to the Jackson Creek exit. Turn north from the off ramp onto Jackson Creek Road and drive another 1.6 miles to the National Forest sign. Find somewhere to park on Jackson Creek Road. Following the National Forest sign, walk up the road 0.4 miles until it dead ends at Whispering Trails. The trail is on your left (north).

Skiing: Ski past the gate and along the road beside a few farm buildings and hay fields. After 0.4 miles cross first one cattle guard, and then another at 0.5 miles. After crossing the third cattle guard at 0.8 miles the fields end and an open sage landscape begins.

At 1.1 miles the sage begins to be interspersed with more conifers, especially near the creek and on the hill across the creek. The road remains fairly flat until 1.8 miles where it rises a little above the creek.

At 3.1 miles you hit an intersection. The road to the left climbs a little and then splits into two roads—both of which end within a couple miles.

Follow the main road straight ahead until you reach a sharp hairpin turn to the right at 4.1 miles. This is our turn around point.

With Kids: This easy, fairly flat ski along a road should be manageable for most kids.

Taking it Further: The road climbs up the hillside and eventually makes a 4.5 mile loop.

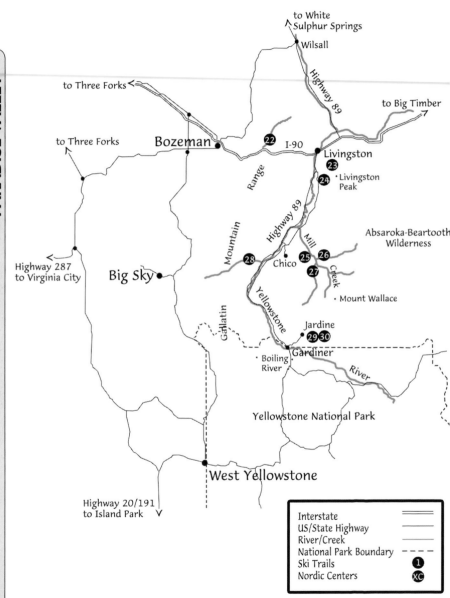

PARADISE VALLEY

This wide glacially formed valley is dissected length-wise by the Yellowstone River, which flows north from Yellowstone Lake in the heart of Yellowstone National Park. To the west, the Gallatin Range rolls up from the river, the highest peaks hidden from most places on the valley floor. To the east, the Absaroka Mountains jut ruggedly into the sky providing a spectacular backdrop to a drive through the valley.

Most of the tours in this book are in the Absaroka Mountains. There is some debate as to whether or not this most-used and locally known name for the range is appropriate. Geologists have long referred to the range as the "North and South Snowy Blocks", and others refer to it as the "Western Beartooths". A peak into the geology confirms that "Western Beartooths" is most accurate, but since these mountains are most popularly known as the "Absaroka Range" (pronounced Ab-zorka), that's what this book uses. And since this book does not cover tours in the real Absarokas (just south in Wyoming) there shouldn't be too much confusion.

The tours in this book avoid the steep trails that crawl up the range, and focus on the mellower trails and roads. Also included, is one trail on the east side of the Gallatin Range—Big Creek Trail. If the Travel Plan put forth by the Forest Service remains as it is currently written, there may be more cross-country skiing opportunities in the future. See page 15 for details.

PARADISE VALLEY

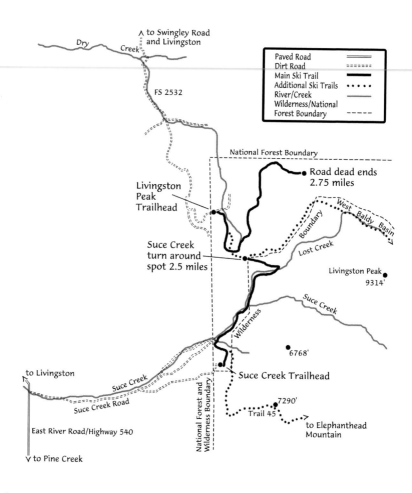

Dry Creek

to Swingley Road and Livingston

FS 2532

National Forest Boundary

Road dead ends 2.75 miles

Livingston Peak Trailhead

Boundary

West Baldy Basin

Lost Creek

Suce Creek turn around spot 2.5 miles

Livingston Peak 9314'

Suce Creek

Wilderness

6768'

to Livingston

Suce Creek

Suce Creek Trailhead

Suce Creek Road

National Forest and Wilderness Boundary

7290'

Trail 45

to Elephanthead Mountain

East River Road/Highway 540

to Pine Creek

Paved Road
Dirt Road
Main Ski Trail
Additional Ski Trails
River/Creek
Wilderness/National Forest Boundary

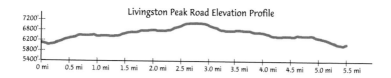

Livingston Peak Road Elevation Profile

7200'
6800'
6200'
5800'
5400'

0 mi   0.5 mi   1.0 mi   1.5 mi   2.0 mi   2.5 mi   3.0 mi   3.5 mi   4.0 mi   4.5 mi   5.0 mi   5.5 mi

23 : Livingston Peak Road

Distance: 5.5 miles round trip

Elevation Gain: 800 feet

Topo Maps: USGS: Livingston Peak
Beartooth Pub: "Absaroka/Beartooth Wilderness"

Trail Report: Depending on the winter and daily weather, the starting point for this tour will vary. Regardless, the ski along the road is mellow, pretty and gains views the higher you go. This tour doesn't go to Livingston Peak, but uses that trailhead.

If you park and ski before getting to the trailhead, stay on the road as it passes through private land.

Getting There: From Main St. in Livingston head east on Park St. for 2.4 miles. Turn right on Swingley Road and drive 2.3 miles to Forest Service Road 2532—signed as National Forest Access. Turn right. Follow the dirt road 0.7 miles where it turns left. After another 4 miles the road begins to climb; this is a good place to park and ski if there is a lot of snow. Otherwise continue to the road's end and trailhead at 7 miles.

Snowshoe Hare Tracks.
Photo © Mariann Van Den Elzen.

PARADISE VALLEY

Skiing: From the trailhead, ski along a timber access road through different stages of logged Douglas-fir trees. Some areas are almost old growth while other areas have been clear cut and are filling in with 3 to 4 foot trees.

After 0.75 miles a trail sign points to the right and to the West Baldy Basin Trail, also accessed from the Suce Creek Trailhead. Continue on the road, enjoying the views.

The road gradually climbs until it dead ends at 2.75 miles. Turn around here and glide quickly back to your vehicle.

With Kids: This trail is a good bet for kids as the incline is easy enough on the way up, but a fun glide on the way down with plenty of room for snowplowing and stopping. The road is conducive to pulling a sled or kid carrier.

Snowshoeing: From the trailhead, take the side trail to the left and cut across the big bend in the road, meeting the road at the West Baldy Basin Trail sign. Follow the "Taking it Further" directions.

Taking it Further: From the West Baldy Basin Trail sign, head steeply down the Suce Creek Trail (and make a through-ski if you can leave a vehicle at the Suce Creek Trailhead) or ski up to the left. From this direction it is possible to access the spur to Livingston Peak.

Noteworthy Views: Canyon Mountain (known as the Wineglass) and the Bangtail Mountains are visible from the early part of the trail. Further along, peak through the trees for vistas of the Crazy Mountains.

On the ski down, Livingston Peak comes into sight, as well as another unnamed, but prominent knob.

24 : Suce Creek Trail

See Map on Page 90

Distance: 5 miles round trip

Elevation Gain: 1,090 feet

Topo Maps: USGS: Livingston Peak & Brisbin
Beartooth Pub: "Absaroka/Beartooth Wilderness"

Trail Report: This trail gets little use given its proximity to Livingston and is a hidden gem. The trail skirts through mixed conifers and follows Suce Creek, then Lost Creek.

Getting There: From Livingston, head south on Highway 89 for 3 miles. Turn left on East River Road and continue another 2.7 miles. Turn left again, on Suce Creek Rd, marked by a street sign as well as a brown National Forest sign. Follow the dirt and gravel road 1.5 miles to another Forest Service access sign and turn right.

From this junction it is 1.5 miles to the trailhead, but you may need to park along the side of the road a little ways up and ski to the trailhead. Because it passes through private property, be sure to stay on the road.

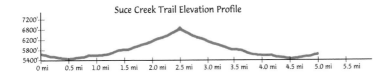

Suce Creek Trail Elevation Profile

Skiing: Leaving the trailhead parking area, ski south through an open meadow to a gate. After passing through the gate, the trail enters forest. Soon after, a trail sign points to West Baldy Basin, straight ahead (and North Fork Deep Creek behind you and to the right). Ski straight ahead and begin the decent to a creek crossing.

The ski down is quick, but with good snow coverage, there is some room for snowplowing. Cross the creek (a tributary of Suce Creek) on the bridge and turn right, following an old road. Suce Creek is to the left. Ski up the gently ascending valley.

At 0.6 miles from the first creek crossing, you will cross Suce Creek and ski up the right side of Lost Creek (dry). In less than a 1.5 miles, cross Lost Creek—now with flowing water—and traverse up the side of a rocky mountain until reaching a gate and a Wilderness Boundary sign, about 0.3 miles further. Enjoy views into the Absarokas and across the Paradise Valley before returning to the trailhead the way you came.

Snowshoeing: Follow the skiing directions until arriving at the trail sign. Instead of heading towards West Baldy Basin at the trail sign, turn right and head up the hill towards North Fork Deep Creek. The trail is uphill the whole way through mixed conifer forests. From several ridges a view into the Absaroka Range is afforded.

Nature Notes: Ruffed Grouse can sometimes be seen along this trail, especially after the first creek crossing. These grouse eat weed seeds and grow special comb-like structures (called pectinations) on the sides of their feet to help them walk on top of the snow.

Taking it Further: From our turn around point you can continue towards Livingston Peak (to the right) or meet up with the Livingston Peak Trail (straight ahead) described on page 91.

Montana: Home to great ski trails and even better marksmen. Trail marker from Suce Creek.

What's in a Name?

The names of peaks, towns and trails in the Livingston area mostly date back to early explorers and settlers, and even earlier to the original inhabitants. Some of the names—like the Crazy Mountains—leave more to the imagination than others.

Crazy Mountains

The name for this island range better known as "The Crazies" is somewhat debated. Some people claim that it was originally called "The Crazy Woman Mountains" after a woman who got left behind as she moved west along the Bozeman Trail with her family. She went insane and lived out the remainder of her days in a cabin, refusing to see or have contact with anyone.

The other possibility (and the more likely one) is that the Absaroka (Crow) Indians called the range "The Crazy Mountains" because that is where they went for vision quests. In this case, "crazy" means "magical" or "mystical" rather than insane.

Livingston

In 1882 the Northern Pacific Railroad deemed what would become Livingston a good spot for a town to service and restock the trains before they headed over Bozeman Pass. The town was originally named "Clark City" for William Clark who passed through here with the Corps of Discovery in 1806. The name of the town and the peak that rises overhead was changed to honor Crawford Livingston, the Director of the Northern Pacific.

Gardiner and Gardner River

The town of Gardiner and the Gardner River, which flows through part of the town, have two different spellings because they were named after two different people. The town was named after a railroad employee.

The Gardner River was named after mountain man Johnson Gardner who first trapped beaver at "Gardner's Hole" several miles away. Yellowstone historian Aubrey Haines called Gardner an "illiterate, often brutal trapper."

PARADISE VALLEY

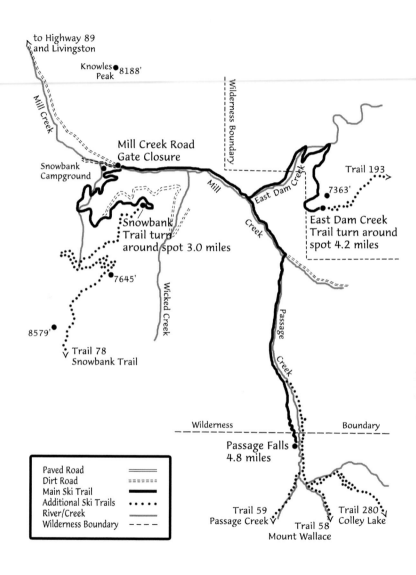

to Highway 89
and Livingston

Knowles ● 8188'
Peak

Mill Creek

Mill Creek Road
Gate Closure

Snowbank
Campground

Wilderness Boundary

Mill

Creek

East Dam Creek

Trail 193

● 7363'

East Dam Creek
Trail turn around
spot 4.2 miles

Snowbank
Trail turn
around spot 3.0 miles

● 7645'

Wicked Creek

8579' ●

Trail 78
Snowbank Trail

Passage

Creek

Wilderness — — — — Boundary

Passage Falls
4.8 miles

Paved Road
Dirt Road
Main Ski Trail
Additional Ski Trails
River/Creek
Wilderness Boundary

Trail 59
Passage Creek

Trail 58
Mount Wallace

Trail 280
Colley Lake

Mill Creek

Trail Report: Mill Creek is the largest drainage in the Absaroka Mountains and provides a series of good skiing trails. This multiple-use area is frequented by snowmobiles, dogsleds and skiers, but is often uncrowded.

There is a sledding hill on the north side of the parking area, which makes this a good destination for kids (or folks who are kids at heart).

Getting There: From Livingston, drive just over 15 miles south on Highway 89 to Mill Creek Rd. (between mile markers 38 and 37). Turn left and travel 11.25 miles until the plowed road ends at a gate (the gate is locked on January 1st, before that you can drive as far as conditions allow). Park in the plowed area on the left.

Nature Notes: Lynx tracks have been found in this area. In 2001, the Canada Lynx was listed as a federally threatened species under the Endangered Species Act, but winter snow track surveys show there is a healthy population of lynx in Montana.

Mill Creek.
Photo © Hannah Sexton.

PARADISE VALLEY

Snowshoeing in the Absarokas

There are many trails in the Absarokas that are ideal for snowshoeing. Grab a map to locate these gems.

South Fork Deep Creek Trail—10.8 miles round trip

This trail starts out on an open sagebrush-filled hillside, switchbacking up to the treeline. After entering the forest, the trail skirts along side Deep Creek (one of the prettiest little creeks around) and then crosses the creek on a bridge. From here the trail climbs above the creek. Eventually, the trail reaches a pass along the Absaroka Crest with excellent views at about 5.4 miles.

Pine Creek Trail—2 miles round trip

This might be the most popular trail in the Absarokas. Even in winter it sees lots of use from hikers, snowshoers and ice climbers. From the end of the Pine Creek Campground, follow the trail 0.25 miles to a junction with the George Lake Trail. Continue straight through the forest and cross Pine Creek on a large bridge. The trail climbs gently to Pine Creek Falls at one mile. The falls are spectacular, so bring a camera. The trail crosses the bridge and continues steeply to Pine Creek Lake at about 5 miles.

East Fork Mill Creek Trail—mileage varies

This trail is narrow and not a great place for cross-country skis (trust me on this one), although backcountry skiers use it. The trail climbs up and down through dense woods, but doesn't gain much elevation for the first 5 miles. At 5 miles there is a junction with one trail heading 4 miles to the top of a scenic pass and the main trail continuing to Silver Pass, approximately 12 miles from the trailhead.

South Fork Sixmile Trail—mileage varies

The first mile the trail crosses the creek several times. At one mile the trail appears to head into a meadow towards an outfitter camp, but you should cross the creek again to the north. The trail generally follows the drainage up hill, staying above the creek, but crosses several side drainages. These side creeks are pretty inconsequential in winter. Eventually the trail tops out at the divide above the north fork of Sixmile Creek.

25 : Snowbank Road

See Map on Page 96

Distance: 2 to 6 miles round trip

Elevation Gain: 1,175 feet

Topo Maps: USGS: Knowles Peak
Beartooth Pub: "Absaroka/Beartooth Wilderness"

Trail Report: This tour (on a dirt road) winds through clear cuts and heavily treed areas as it gently climbs to an area with great views.

Skiing: Ski past the gate on the road and immediately turn right toward the Snowbank Campground. Cross the bridge and take the left, or upper, road. Follow this logging road uphill 1 to 3 miles through spruce, fir and pine forest.

Between 1.5 and 2 miles the road splits, stay right. Almost immediately the road splits again, stay left.

There is no real destination to this tour, so turn around whenever the mood strikes. After 3 miles we'll end this tour. Return the way you came. The ski down is fast and fun, but technically easy and requires little effort on the skiers' part.

With Kids: This is a wide, fun tour, perfect for kids. If they are expert enough to control a sled, this is a fun place for kids to ski up and sled down the straight-ish sections.

Taking it Further: From our turn around point, the road continues another 1.5 miles before turning into a summer hiking trail. There are also several other roads that spur off the main road which could be used for further exploration.

Noteworthy Views: Skiing through a timber harvest affords views of the Mill Creek Valley, and eventually, across the Paradise Valley into the Gallatin Range. Towards the top of the hill, look across the Mill Creek drainage to spot Arrow Peak and into the Absarokas for a view of Mount Cowen and The Pyramid.

PARADISE VALLEY

Skiing the Snowbank Road.

East Dam Creek Trail Elevation Profile

26 : East Dam Creek Trail

See Map on Page 96

Distance: 8.4 miles round trip

Elevation Gain: 1,490 feet

Topo Maps: USGS: Knowles Peak
Beartooth Pub: "Absaroka/Beartooth Wilderness"

Trail Report: The first part of the tour travels along a road used by skiers, snowmobilers, walkers and dogsledders, but is often uncrowded as it parallels Mill Creek. After a short jaunt on the road, a trail heads to the north through conifers and meadows.

Skiing: Ski past the gate and up the road 1.6 miles. Look for the Forest Service sign on the right, the big, fenced dirt pile on the left and the trailhead sign just beyond the dirt pile.

The narrow trail begins just behind the trailhead sign and climbs through big trees including spruce, fir and Rocky Mountain Juniper. Ironically, the trail widens into an old logging road at the Wilderness boundary and 0.6 miles from the East Dam Creek trailhead. From here, there are nice views of a sheer rock outcrop.

The trail then sweeps widely to the right and continues winding and climbing the side of the hill. Keep skiing up, until 4.2 miles from the parking area or where the trail turns east at an open, windblown hillside. The tour ends here, but the trail continues around the mountain and into the Absaroka Range.

The return ski is quick and easy until reaching the Wilderness sign. From there to the trailhead it can be very fast if there isn't much new snow. Since the trail is narrow, maintain a controlled speed if possible.

With Kids: The ski along the road is easy, but the trail is a bit hairy, with no room to slow or stop near the bottom, so stick to the road and ski as far as little legs want to go.

Snowshoeing: If you don't mind the 1.6 mile trudge along the road to the trailhead, the East Dam Creek Trail is nice for snowshoeing, with many possible offshoots for the adventurous explorer.

Noteworthy Views: Across the valley, huge clear cuts fill the view with rugged Absaroka peaks beyond. To the northwest, Knowles Peak dominates the viewshed.

Rigby enjoying Passage Falls.

PARADISE VALLEY

27 : Passage Creek Falls Trail

See Map on Page 96

Distance: 9.6 miles round trip

Elevation Gain: 700 feet

Topo Maps: USGS: Knowles Peak, The Pyramid, Mount Wallace
Beartooth Pub: "Absaroka/Beartooth Wilderness"

Trail Report: The first part of the tour travels along a road used by skiers, snowmobilers, walkers and dogsledders, but is often uncrowded as it parallels Mill Creek.

The trail skirts through trees, small meadows and past a volcanic scree slope before heading up a short hill—then down another—to a majestic waterfall.

Skiing: Ski past the gate and up the road 2.4 miles. Look for a big pull-through parking area on the right with a trailhead sign at the south end.

Ski across Mill Creek on the wooden bridge, and soon after cross Passage Creek on another bridge. At 1.6 miles from the Passage Creek Trailhead a trail veers to the right while the main trail crosses a bridge to the left.

Follow the right trail to the top of a steep, short hill and a view of open meadows on the other side. The trail turns to the left and then drops down eight narrow, switchbacks. Leave your skis here and walk down to the waterfall, or brave the decent and ski it. The trail ends abruptly, so be prepared to stop quickly and without much room. Ski back the way you came.

Passage Creek Falls Trail Elevation Profile

With Kids: The first 1.6 miles from the trailhead are fairly flat and mellow. For kids with good endurance—the whole ski is pretty long—this is a nice tour. Hike the hill in both directions to avoid nasty spills.

Taking it Further: From the bridge at 1.6 miles, the left trail continues another 0.4 miles before splitting into two trails. The right trail follows the East Fork Wallace Creek and eventually climbs to the saddle below Mt. Wallace (10, 697). The left trail climbs a ridge and then descends to Mill Creek Road east of the Passage Falls Trailhead. Both tours require advanced skiing skills and equipment.

PARADISE VALLEY

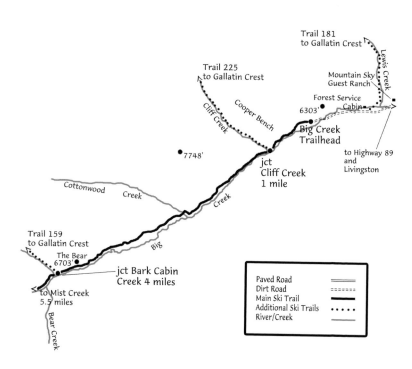

Trail 181
to Gallatin Crest

Lewis Creek

Trail 225
to Gallatin Crest

Mountain Sky
Guest Ranch

Forest Service
Cabin

6303'

Cliff Creek

Cooper Bench

Big Creek
Trailhead

7748'

jct
Cliff Creek
1 mile

to Highway 89
and
Livingston

Cottonwood   Creek

Creek

Trail 159
to Gallatin Crest

The Bear
6703'

Big

jct Bark Cabin
Creek 4 miles

to Mist Creek
5.5 miles

Bear Creek

Paved Road	———
Dirt Road	=======
Main Ski Trail	▬▬▬
Additional Ski Trails	• • • •
River/Creek	∿∿∿

Big Creek Trail Elevation Profile

7400'
7000'
6600'
6200'
5800'

0 mi   1.0 mi   2.0 mi   3.0 mi   4.0 mi   5.0 mi   6.0 mi   7.0 mi   8.0 mi   9.0 mi   10.0 mi   11.0 mi

28 : Big Creek Trail

Distance: 2 miles to Cliff Creek Trail; 8 miles to Bark Cabin
Trail; 11 miles round trip to Mist Creek Trail

Elevation Gain: 0 at Cliff Creek Trail; 200 feet at Bark Cabin;
1,100 feet at Mist Creek Trail

Topo Maps: USGS: Lewis Creek & The Sentinel
Beartooth Pub: "Absaroka/Beartooth Wilderness"

Trail Report: This narrow, but mellow trail follows Big Creek as it
larks down the valley. Often the east side of the Gallatin Range doesn't
receive nearly as much snow as the west side or the Absarokas across the
Paradise Valley. But, if the snow is adequate for skiing, you'll almost be
guaranteed of having the place to yourself.

In the summer there are numerous cows in the creek and the trail is
frequently used for trail rides by Mountain Sky Guest Ranch. Winter
snows cover the abundant cow trails and render the trail very pretty.

Getting There: From Livingston, drive south on Highway 89 to Big
Creek Road—28.6 miles. Turn right and drive 3.4 miles to where the
road forks; stay left towards the Big Creek Station. It's another 1.6 miles
to a parking area for Mountain Sky Guest Ranch on the left and a bridge
crossing Big Creek. Either park here or drive another 1.1 miles to the
trailhead parking and a sign for Big Creek Trailhead.

Skiing: Walk up the steep (and very short) embankment to a cattle gate.
On the other side of the gate follow the Big Creek Trail on the left.
In several places cows have made trails down to the creek (they aren't
around in the winter), so ignore these and stay on the main trail above,
and parallel to the creek.

After 1 mile you'll reach a signed turnoff to the Cliff Creek Trail.
Continue on the Big Creek Trail to the Bark Cabin Trail at 4 miles or the
Mist Creek Trail at 5.5 miles. Turn around wherever the mood strikes.

Snowshoeing: I haven't fully investigated the snowshoeing options in
the area, however there are several other trails that leave from the same
parking area—Cooper Bench Trail, Lewis Creek and Trail 183. These
likely all provide great snowshoeing opportunities.

Taking it Further: The Big Creek Trail travels many miles back
into the Gallatin Range and links up with several other trails. Many of
these trails will be difficult to find in the winter, but for someone with a
GPS unit and the proclivity to spend a night or two winter camping, the
possibilities are numerous.

PARADISE VALLEY

Bear Creek Trail System

Trail Report: Driving through Gardiner, it's hard to believe there can be enough snow within a few miles for even halfway decent skiing, but the trails above Jardine often have some of the best snow in the area.

There are a variety of great trails and terrain in the Bear Creek Trail System, from level roads to steep slopes, and the numerous trails can be linked up to create a number of great skiing experiences.

Getting There: From Livingston, drive 51 miles south on Highway 89 to Gardiner. Just before crossing the Yellowstone Bridge veer left towards Jardine. Follow the red dirt road 5.4 miles to Jardine and then turn right over the bridge in the middle of town. Take Bear Creek Road up 1.7 miles and veer left into the parking area.

Nature Notes: You probably won't see any bears in the Bear Creek area, at least in the winter. From time to time, however, bears will emerge from their winter den if the weather is warm and amiable. These bears will look for food, eat, and then return to their hibernation. Both black and grizzly bears live in the area.

Bear Creek Trail System.

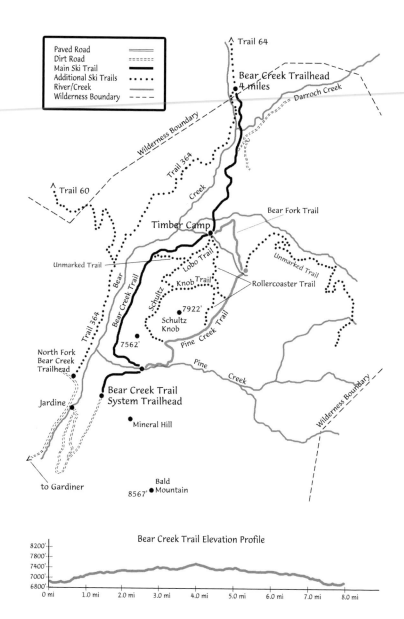

PARADISE VALLEY

Paved Road
Dirt Road
Main Ski Trail
Additional Ski Trails
River/Creek
Wilderness Boundary

↑ Trail 64

Bear Creek Trailhead
4 miles

Darroch Creek

Wilderness Boundary

Trail 364

Creek

↑ Trail 60

Bear Fork Trail

Timber Camp

Unmarked Trail

Lobo Trail

Unmarked Trail

Bear

Bear Creek Trail

Knob Trail

Rollercoaster Trail

Trail 364

Schultz

7922'

Pine Creek Trail

Schultz
Knob

7562'

North Fork
Bear Creek
Trailhead

Pine

Creek

Jardine

Wilderness Boundary

Bear Creek Trail
System Trailhead

Mineral Hill

to Gardiner

Bald
8567' ● Mountain

Bear Creek Trail Elevation Profile

8200'
7800'
7400'
7000'
6800'

0 mi   1.0 mi   2.0 mi   3.0 mi   4.0 mi   5.0 mi   6.0 mi   7.0 mi   8.0 mi

29 : Bear Creek Trail

Distance: 8 miles round trip

Elevation Gain: 225 feet

Topo Maps: USGS: Gardiner & Ash Mountain
Beartooth Pub: "Absaroka/Beartooth Wilderness"

Trail Report: This tour follows the Forest Service road to its terminus at the Bear Creek trailhead, passing through fir, spruce and pine forest.

The groomed and tracked trail is also used by snowmobiles to access the backcountry, but there never seem to be too many at once, and less on weekdays. The Bear Creek Trail is a good entry point for loops with other trails in the area.

Skiing: From the parking area head back up to the road and continue in the direction you were driving (left). Ski the gently inclining road as it widely traverses around Schultz Knob. After 2 miles, Timber Camp appears to the left.

The main road continues another 2 miles to the Bear Creek trailhead near the Wilderness boundary. This is our turn around point.

With Kids: This is a great trail for kids or beginning skiers. The road is fairly flat, wide and sometimes groomed for track skiing. This is also an easy trail on which to pull a sled or kid carrier.

The Timber Camp is a big, open area, perfect for picnics, snowball fights and snow sculpting. If there are snowmobiles at Timber Camp, ski off to the right before reaching the camp into one of the many open glades.

Snowshoeing: The road itself isn't much fun for snowshoeing, although perfect for a fitness snowshoer looking to run or work out. Off the road, however are lots of open glades that make for super snowshoeing.

Taking it Further: Just beyond Timber Camp is another Forest Service road to the right. This road can be used to access the Bear Fork, Rollercoaster and Lobo trails creating several loops.

Noteworthy Views: In the southwest views into Yellowstone National Park are dominated by the Mammoth Terraces, Bunsen Peak, 10,336 foot Mt. Holmes and 10,992 foot Electric Peak. Bunsen Peak was named after Robert Bunsen, the inventor of the Bunsen burner found in almost every science lab.

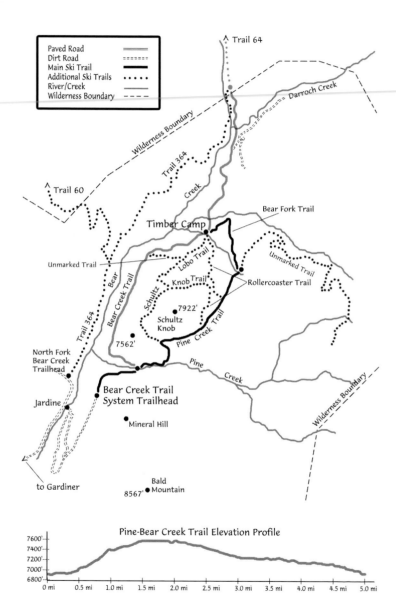

PARADISE VALLEY

↑ Trail 64

Paved Road
Dirt Road
Main Ski Trail
Additional Ski Trails
River/Creek
Wilderness Boundary

Darroch Creek

Wilderness Boundary

Trail 364

↑ Trail 60

Creek

Bear Fork Trail

Timber Camp

Unmarked Trail

Lobo Trail

Unmarked Trail

Knob Trail

Rollercoaster Trail

Bear

Bear Creek Trail

Schultz

7922'

Schultz
Knob

Pine Creek Trail

7562'

Trail 364

North Fork
Bear Creek
Trailhead

Pine

Creek

Wilderness Boundary

Jardine

Bear Creek Trail
System Trailhead

Mineral Hill

to Gardiner

Bald
8567' ● Mountain

Pine-Bear Creek Trail Elevation Profile

7600'
7400'
7200'
7000'
6800'

0 mi   0.5 mi   1.0 mi   1.5 mi   2.0 mi   2.5 mi   3.0 mi   3.5 mi   4.0 mi   4.5 mi   5.0 mi

30 : Pine Creek & Bear Forks Trails

Distance: 5 miles out and back;
            4.5 miles if looped with Bear Creek Trail

Elevation Gain: 750 feet

Topo Maps: USGS: Gardiner & Ash Mountain
            Beartooth Pub: "Absaroka/Beartooth Wilderness"

Trail Report: These trails wind in and out of meadows and forested areas and provide nice views as well as interesting scenery.

Skiing: From the parking area ski back up to the road and continue in the direction you were driving (left). As you round the first corner look for the wooden Pine Creek Trail sign on the right.

Follow the steep trail up towards Schultz Knob for 0.5 miles before the climb begins to mellow.

The Pine Creek Trail ends abruptly after 1.5 miles at the signed Bear Fork Trail, actually a forest service road. Turn left and glide all the way down to the Bear Creek Trail at 2.25 miles. Turn left and follow the Bear Creek Trail back to the parking area, return the way you came, or climb back up one of the other trails.

Additional Note: For those who do not love to herringbone or don't have skins for their skis, an easier way to ski this loop is to begin on the Bear Creek Trail and catch the Bear Fork Trail about 2 miles up at the Timber Camp. The last 0.5 miles will be steep and fast, but the slope is wide open, with plenty of room to turn, traverse or take a header.

Snowshoeing: There are lots of options for snowshoers from the Pine Creek Trailhead. Almost immediately, the opportunities open up in every direction. Or parallel the ski trails in the above directions.

Taking it Further: Just before the steep climb from the Pine Creek Trailhead ends, the Schultz Knob Trail takes off on the left, traverses the Knob in 1.3 miles and meets up again with the Pine Creek Trail just beyond the 1 mile mark.

About halfway up the Pine Creek Trail, the Rollercoaster Trail veers off to the left. This fun route drops about 1 mile to the Bear Creek Trail.